MIRA...
FAITH
— AND —
GOD'S
— WILL —

By
GRAHAM FITZPATRICK

SOVEREIGN WORLD

MIRACLES FAITH and GOD'S WILL

The Good News Version of the Bible was used because of its simple, easy-to-read English. This makes this book easier to read for clergy who receive this book in countries where English is only a second language. But because the Good News Version sometimes uses wording that is so simple that it diverges slightly from the original Greek text, the Amplified Version became necessary. The Amplified is over-wordy in parts, so it was necessary to use the less wordy Revised Standard Version which some argue to be closer to the original Greek than the Good News Version. The Authorized Version was used a small number of times also. Throughout the book, some of the words of the Scripture references have been capitalized by the author for emphasis.

ISBN 1 5240 022 6

"This book is not your textbook. The Holy Scriptures are your textbook. Only the Holy Scriptures are totally inspired by God.

Only those parts of this or any other religious book that are in agreement with the teachings of the Holy Scriptures should be accepted by a reader as being true. Never forget this!"

OTHER BOOKS BY THE SAME AUTHOR:

How To Recognize God's Voice.
Keys To Knowing God Better.
What Devotion To God And Holiness Is Not.
Highest Authority: Church, Scripture, Or Tradition?
Miracles—And If It Be Thy Will.
Are The Popes The Infallible Highest Authority?

ANY ENQUIRIES ABOUT THESE BOOKS SHOULD BE SENT TO:

Spiritual Growth Publications
P.O. Box 228
Fairy Meadow
N.S.W. 2519
Australia

Contents

INTRODUCTION

These days, when people think of miracles, they usually think of praying for the healing of human bodies. God miraculously heals many people. But this book is **not about miracles of healing.** Nor is it about casting demons out of people.

Neither is this book primarily about those types of miracles that God in His Scriptures promises to all believers—the giving to us of His salvation, His Holy Spirit, His wisdom, His strength to live our daily lives properly, the presence of the Lord Jesus' love within us and many similar things. There are many good books written about these things already.

Neither is this book about praying for church revival or praying that God will convict specific unbelievers of their sin, lack of love for and lack of devotion to the Lord Jesus Christ. It is God's will for His churches to be revived continually and to have His Spirit convict unbelievers very heavily of their sin (see John 16:7-9, 1 Thessalonians 1:5). Therefore, He is always pleased for us to pray in faith for Him to do these things.

This book is mainly about the types of miracles that **are not specifically promised** in the Scriptures to all believers. These include the **less spectacular** to the human physical eyes, ears and so on—such as praying for a specific job at a specific place or that we will marry a specific person.

It also includes the **more spectacular** such as running faster than horses as Elijah did, walking on water like Peter did, being carried by the Spirit through the air for 30 miles or more like Philip was and trusting God for drought like Elijah did.

We will also learn how to trust God for such miracles. We will see how we can be absolutely certain whether God will perform a specific miracle. We will also examine some false teachings about praying for miracles that are being accepted by some churchgoers at present. Sadly, some of these false teachings are being taught by some of the most popular Pentecostal and Charismatic Christian television preachers in the United States at the present time and have been uncritically accepted by many godly ministers, pastors and lay people in many nations. Others of these errors are taught by many Protestants, Catholics and Orthodox.

The expression "a miracle of God" can be defined in part as the **supernatural intervention** of God into the natural realm. It is God intervening in the affairs of the human race, animals, plants, the Earth, the Sun, the Moon, the stars and other natural things. A "miracle of God" can also involve God's supernatural intervention in the realms of angels and demons. It can also refer to the various ways in which God influences the spirit of a human being. Miracles are possible because God is a **personal Being** and has **unlimited power** which He can use to influence anything or anyone.

The above is a **general** definition. It is difficult to be overly specific when defining the expression "a miracle of God", because a number of good reasons can be given to suggest that such things as rainfall, the wind, the conception and birth of a child and similar things can also be regarded as "miracles of God". Therefore, to avoid taking too many pages to define it, the above general definition will be sufficient.

Since the Bible teaches that Satan and demons can perform miracles also (see Matthew 24:24, Acts 16:16-18, 2 Thessalonians 2:8-9, Revelation 13:11-15, and 16:14), we must be very careful to **test** all miracles to see if they are really from God. A so-called "miracle of God" will not be from Him if it encourages us to **put in first place in our minds** some person, angel, statue, picture or some natural thing other than God Himself. 1 Corinthians 10:31 shows this. So does John 16:14 which infers that the Holy Spirit will not glorify anyone or anything other than the Lord Jesus Christ.

A so-called "miracle of God" will also not be from God if it occurs in a way contrary to the teachings of the Scriptures or if it encourages us to act in ways contrary to the teachings of the Scriptures (see Deuteronomy 13:1-3). The

Scriptures express **how God acts, thinks** and **feels** (see 2 Timothy 3:16, Luke 24:27, 44-45, Acts 17:2-3, 24:14, Romans 15:4, 1 Corinthians 14:37-38, 2 Peter 1:20-21, 3:15-16).

You may write a book expressing what you think and how you act in various situations. If I read your book thoroughly, I would come to understand your character, thoughts and actions. Even though I have never physically met you, if someone else came to me claiming to be you, after observing this person's behaviour, and listening to his words, I would know if he were you or not.

The same principle applies to "miracles of God". God is not going to show in His Scriptures how He thinks and acts, and then do things contrary to this when performing a miracle.

PREFACE

Before beginning to study how to trust the Lord to perform miracles which are not specifically promised in His Scriptures, we must remember:

- never to be more interested in His miracles than what we are in Him. We must **love God more** than **anything else** including His miraculous intervention in our lives (see Matthew 22:37-38).

- never to seek to have God perform miracles for us so that other people will praise us or so they will give us money. Read 2 Kings Chapter 5 and Acts 8:18-24, to see how the prophet Elisha's servant Gehazi and Simon the Samaritan occult leader wished to use God's miracle-working power for such evil purposes. If we are wishing to use His miracle-working power because of self-centredness or pride, this is **an enormous evil.**

- to aim always to see God put in **His rightful place of honour** in our thoughts and actions and in the thoughts and actions of as many other people as possible. We should aim to put God **first** in all things in our lives—in our words, our thoughts, our actions, in our obedience to Him, in our eating and drinking and in **all** other spiritual and natural things. This is what it means to glorify God in everything we do, as 1 Corinthians 10:31 commands us all to do.

1
God's Character And Will

What God wants is always best for us—in the short term and in the long run. The expression "according to God's will" sounds very negative and discouraging to many people. Their mental picture of praying "according to God's will" is of prayer which is imprisoned and greatly restricted. Some are convinced that the will of God has so many limits and restrictions on it that it is of little use asking God for anything. Others are afraid to try to pray according to God's will because they think that God desires always to give them **what is worst for them.** They imagine that God wishes to make their lives as miserable or unhappy as possible. Others may not be as extreme as this, but they still don't think that God's will for their lives is best for them.

How misled they are! They have a very wrong understanding of **what His will is** and of **what His character is like.** They fail to realize that praying for miracles is limited **far more** by **failing to pray according to the will of God** than it is praying according to His will.

MISUNDERSTANDING OF GOD'S KNOWLEDGE

Our problem is that **we are often content to have less than God's best.** If we were only able to look at our lives with the unlimited wisdom that God has, we would see how silly we are when we think that our plans for our lives are better than His. He knows everything that you or I are going to think even before we think it (see Revelation 17:8, Psalm 139:4). Even though He does not cause every event that occurs in the universe, His mind is so awesome in ability that it knows every event that is going to happen in the future before it happens.

Before the Earth even existed, He knew the exact time we would wake up today and exactly which clothes we would put on. He knew how many words we would speak today, how many times we would blink our eyes and what we would eat today. This is not fate or destiny, because God doesn't cause everything that happens. He has given a free will to us with which we make many decisions. He doesn't force us to make sinful decisions. However, His mind is so incredible, that it could know before the Earth existed every decision, good or bad, that we were going to make. This is why it is foolish for us to think that we could know what is best for us, better than what God could: our limited minds often can't even remember what someone told us yesterday, yet we still imagine that we know what is best for us.

We forget that God created minds, bodies, marriage, children, husbands, wives, friends, food, sex, education, government, the raw materials from which houses, clothes, televisions, musical instruments and so on are made. Since He created these things, He should know how they should be used and related to properly. Satan tricks many people into believing that he is the "sex expert", the expert in helping young men and women find their marriage partner and the expert in other areas of life. But Satan is not the expert in any of these areas. God is the expert.

God's will is so **incredibly good** for every individual, that a person who asks for things according to it, will find himself or herself blessed beyond his or her wildest imagination. God **always** wants the best for every individual. When I say "the best", I mean "what He knows in His unlimited knowledge and love is best for each individual".

God's best sometimes corresponds with what a human thinks is best. For example, a man may think that it is best that he gets a new job, which gives him more time to develop his love relationship with his wife and time to help, encourage and teach new Christians. God may see that this is the wisest thing to do also.

Another man may wish to change his job because some of the people there don't like and criticize him often because he is a Christian. This man may think in his limited wisdom that it is best that he leaves. But God may see that really it is best for the man if he stays, learns how to deeply love

14

people who don't like him and learns to not be looking for approval from other people. God in His **unlimited** wisdom may see that the strengthening of this man's character is really better for the man in the **long run,** than him being able in the short term to avoid this criticism and dislike by changing jobs.

In this latter example, God's best differed from what the human thought was best.

Praying according to God's will is one of **the most rewarding** and **sometimes exciting** things that a person can do in his life. It is a life that is sometimes filled with the great joy, peace and love of the Holy Spirit. Also, it often involves the self-sacrifice of time, money and of oneself. It can also lead to much persecution and criticism by non-Christians, Christians-in-name-only, and even some other Christians.

Praying according to God's will is one part of learning more about **intimately knowing** and **loving God more.**

GOD'S CHARACTER

Some people understand how unlimited is God's knowledge and power, but they think that God is probably not willing to use His knowledge and power for them. There are a number of variations to this idea.

Some think that God is too interested in Himself to be concerned about using His wisdom and power to help them. Do you think this? If you do, you don't really understand God's character. God is a totally unselfish Person. He is more interested in the happiness of others than He is in His own. God not only loves you **much more than your mother** or **father**. He also wishes to have a **closer, more intimate** love relationship with you than any good husband and wife have had with each other. God is **kinder, gentler** and **more sympathetic** than the nicest person that you know. Galatians 5:22 tells what sort of character the Holy Spirit has:

> "*But the fruit of the Spirit is love, joy, peace, patience, kindness, goodness, faithfulness, gentleness, self-control....*" (Revised Standard Version)

Since the Holy Spirit and God the Father have the same character, this verse reveals what sort of character the Father has.

Some have been wrongly taught by their minister or priest that they should not trouble the God of the Universe

15

with their so-called unimportant requests. They then feel guilty about asking God to help them or perform miracles for them. This is a wrong concept of God also. Jesus expressed this in Luke 12:6-7 where He said:

"Are not five sparrows sold for two pennies? And [yet] not one of them is forgotten or uncared for in the presence of God. But [even] the very hairs of your head are all numbered. Do not be struck with fear or seized with alarm; you are of greater worth than many [flocks] of sparrows."   (Amplified Version)

If God is very concerned about **minor things** such as these, He is interested in every one of your prayers.

All of us at various stages of our lives have been deceived about God's character. Demons hate us and they hate God. To destroy any love or trust that we may develop towards God, they constantly whisper lies into our minds about God's true character. Some ministers and priests have passed on to us their own false understanding of God's character. God said in Psalm 95:10 about the Israelites who went with Moses out of Egypt:

"It is a people that do err in their heart, and they have NOT KNOWN MY WAYS."   (Authorised Version)

God wishes to perform **more** miracles in many of our lives than we are able to accept from Him. For example, He may wish to have us pray for Him to raise someone from the dead. But because He knows that we may be too proud at present for Him to do this in answer to our prayer, He may not lead us to pray for such things. He does not want to see us fall into evil through pride. So to keep us from falling, He will often wait until we are more humble, before trying to lead us to pray for such things. Some people through refusing to mature in God, may never reach the point where God leads them to pray for such spectacular miracles in the lives of others and see them happen, without falling through pride.

2 Samuel 12:7-8 suggests that God wishes to perform more miracles in our lives than we are ready to accept from Him. When talking to David, God said:

"...I anointed you king of Israel and I delivered you out of the hand of Saul; And I gave you your master's

house, and your master's wives into your bosom, and
I gave you the house of Israel and of Judah; and if
that had been too little, I would HAVE ADDED
THAT MUCH AGAIN."   *(Amplified Version)*

This is God's will: He wants to give us much more than
we know of.

Jesus said similar things about the people of Jerusalem.
He expressed the sadness in God's heart about people not
allowing Him to miraculously do things for them in Matthew
23:37:

"Jerusalem, Jerusalem! You kill the prophets and stone
the messengers God has sent you! How many times I
WANTED to put my arms around all your people,
just as a hen gathers her chicks under her wings, but
YOU WOULD NOT LET ME!"

(Good News Version)

Some may argue that the above two Scriptural references relate only to David and then Jerusalem. But
Ephesians 3:20 also expresses similar things:

"To him who by means of his power working in us is
able to do SO MUCH MORE than we can ever ASK
FOR, or even THINK OF."   *(Good News Version)*

FOOTNOTE:
1. The Chapter "God's True Character" in my book, "KEYS TO
KNOWING GOD BETTER" gives a detailed understanding of God's real
character. Note that my book "KEYS TO GROWING IN HOLINESS"
has been re-named "KEYS TO KNOWING GOD BETTER".

2
The Importance Of
God's Will

God's limitless power is irresistible in heaven and on Earth. It is not like an electric power point though that can be used for any purpose. His power can only be used to achieve purposes approved of by Him.

God will not allow His power to be used to do the will of man. God's power is **only available to accomplish His will.** By limiting His power to prayer requests based on His will, God prevents people from using His Holy Spirit's power for evil, selfish or careless purposes. (A slight qualification to this statement is made in Chapter 9 "Asking Outside of God's Will.")

Some things for which we may wish to ask God, may not really be for our best in the long run. God **loves us too much** to allow His power to be used for things that are not really for our long-term good.

Praying for miracles involves giving ourselves totally over to our God, just as Romans 12:1 says:

> *"I appeal to you therefore, brethren, and beg of you in view of [all] the mercies of God, to make a **decisive dedication of your bodies**—presenting all your **members** and **faculties**—as a **living sacrifice,** holy (devoted, consecrated) and well-pleasing to God, which is your reasonable (rational, intelligent) service and spiritual worship."* (Amplified Version)

This verse includes all of the specific things that we would want Him to do for us. We must commit all our desires to God, asking Him what He wants us to trust Him to do for us.

To find out His will about what specific miracles He wants us to trust Him for, we must do two things.

First, we must be **totally willing** to **do whatever He says.** The reason why many people are not led by God, is that they are not really willing to follow what He tells them to. They are the type of Christian who proudly thinks that they know better than God. As Proverbs 3:5 says, in paraphrased form, we should trust in the Lord and lean not on our own understanding.

How could our small human brains, which cannot understand the notion of infinity, work out things better than a God Who knows everything about everything? It is silly human conceit that makes us believe that we can work out what is best for us. Think how small we are compared with the universe—the universe is small when compared with God.

God will often not tell us what type of prayer request it is His will to answer, unless we have begun to be **willing to only request from Him whatever He tells us to request.**

The second thing we must do in finding God's will about what prayer requests He will answer is to **know** what He **promises to answer.** The Bible is our main source of knowledge of God's will. Unless we search it a lot, we will be in doubt about God's will and will not be able to pray in faith and get answers to our requests.

3
The Importance Of
The Holy Spirit

You may be saying at this point, "I know how to pray in faith about the various promises from the Scriptures until I receive an answer from God. However, since the Bible doesn't give promises specific enough in certain circumstances, then how can I know what God wants me to request of Him in these situations? For example, how can I know whether I'm to trust God to enable me to move to Tokyo, or London, or Cairo, or Dublin, or Belfast? Or how do I know whether God wants me to trust Him to bring about my marriage to John, or Peter, or Fred (if I'm a woman), or Mary, Joan or Helen (if I'm a man)?"

The Bible says that it is mostly God's will for people to marry (see Matthew 19:11-12). Therefore, God promises most people a wife or a husband by a **general** Biblical promise. However, the Bible doesn't give a **specific** promise or verse which says, "You are to marry Fred", or "You are to marry Joan". A Christian cannot ask God to bring about a marriage to Fred or Joan unless the Holy Spirit reveals that this is His will.

A person who desires to pray in true Biblical faith, needs not only to know what God in the Bible reveals that He wants him to request. He also needs to know how to obtain guidance directly from God the Holy Spirit about specific matters of which the **Bible doesn't give such specific guidance.**

The Holy Spirit reveals God's will about these matters mainly through:

- the inner witness (see Romans 8:16, Colossians 3:15, Philippians 4:7)

21

- the still small voice (see 1 Kings 19:12, John 10:27, Isaiah 30:21)
- circumstances (see Matthew 16:2-3, Isaiah 7:10-14 and 37:30-32).

On rarer occasions, He uses dreams, audible voices and other spectacular supernatural means.

GOD NEVER SPEAKS AGAINST WHAT HE HAS WRITTEN

As stated in the Introduction of this book, know clearly that the Holy Spirit will NEVER give us an inner witness or 'still small voice' or a sign or dream and so on that suggests that God is saying something to us contrary to the teachings of His Scriptures. He will **never ever** do this. Remember this while studying the following chapters.

The Scriptures will show if the so-called "guidance" is telling us to do or believe something opposite to or different from what God teaches.

For example, if the so-called "inner voice" tells us to try to communicate with spirits of the dead, we will know that this voice is a demon talking or is merely our own human reasoning. Deuteronomy 18:11 says not to try to talk to the spirits of the dead. THE WRITTEN WORD AND GOD THE HOLY SPIRIT NEVER DISAGREE.

There are too many Christians these days claiming that the Holy Spirit has told them to do something, when He has not. We must be very careful.

This is where the teaching of my own book, "HOW TO RECOGNIZE GOD'S VOICE",[1] is necessary reading for anyone who wishes to know how to obtain direct revelation of the will of God, and how to **distinguish** God's guidance from the thoughts and emotions of his own fleshly mind and from the suggestions placed in his mind by demons. This book should be re-read many times, until deep understanding of how to get guidance from God is obtained. We have to be very careful not to be misled by Satan or our own thoughts and feelings.

Unless we are aiming to become more sensitive to the voice of the Holy Spirit, we will find **great difficulty** in trying to trust God to do things not specifically promised in His Holy Scriptures.

WATCHMAN NEE

Watchman Nee knew some things about the correct way to pray. Nee said that all good prayer requests are based on the following four principles. He said, "The first step is that God conceives a **thought,** which is His will. The second step is that God reveals His will to His children **through the Holy Spirit,** causing them to know that He has a will, a plan, a demand and expectation. The third step is that God's children return His will by praying to Him, for prayer is responding to God's will—if our heart is wholly one with His heart, we will naturally voice in our prayer what He intends to do. And the fourth step is that God will accomplish this very thing."[2]

FOOTNOTES:
1. Graham Fitzpatrick, "HOW TO RECOGNIZE GOD'S VOICE", Spiritual Growth Books, Australia, 1985.
2. Watchman Nee, "LET US PRAY", Christian Fellowship Publishers, 1977, New York, P. 24.

4
Commit Our Decision-Making To Him

Whenever we are seeking to know God's will about something that the Bible does not specifically reveal, we should wait upon the Lord saying something like, "Lord, I'm here and I will listen to Your voice. If You say 'Yes', I will go; if You say 'No', I'm not going. **I don't wish to make decisions for my own benefit,** but to decide according to YOUR DESIRE and WILL. Whether it causes **good** or **trouble** for me, I'm ready to accept your guidance." By this attitude, we show God that we are willing to obey whatever He guides us to do.

At this point of dedication or deep committal to God, usually then or in the following days, weeks or years, He will be willing to guide us as to what we are to **do** or **request of Him.** God usually will not guide us much as a Christian if we are not willing to obey His will constantly, and to forsake our own limited human plans which often only cause us trouble and worry.

The Book of Judges contains many examples of people doing things in Israel based on their own human plans. Judges 17:6 and 21:25 say that in those days, *"every man did what was right in their own eyes."* Because they rarely followed God's will in the time of the Book of Judges, much wickedness, selfishness and suffering occurred at that time. Israel was constantly conquered because they **continually got out of God's will** by "doing what was right in their own eyes".

INNER GUIDANCE FROM GOD'S SPIRIT
Acts 16:6-12 reveals that Paul and Silas were good examples of how God the Holy Spirit wants to guide us, as we

learn to recognize His guidance. In these verses, we see that Paul and Silas constantly obeyed the Holy Spirit's guidance about where to go. The Bible did not specifically tell them to which town God wanted them to go. Therefore, they had to have direct revelations from the Holy Spirit. Note the emphasized parts of the following verses:

> *"And Paul and Silas passed through the territory of Phrygia and Galatia, having been FORBIDDEN BY THE HOLY SPIRIT to proclaim the Word in [the province of] Asia. And when they had come opposite Mysia, they tried to go into Bithynia, but the SPIRIT OF JESUS DID NOT PERMIT THEM. So passing by Mysia, they went down to Troas. [There] a vision appeared to Paul in the night: a man from Macedonia stood ... And when he had seen the vision, we at once endeavoured to go into Macedonia, confidently inferring that God had called us to proclaim the glad tidings (Gospel) to them." (Acts 16:6-10)*
>
> *(Amplified Version)*

Paul and Silas **obeyed** the **leadings of the Holy Spirit** day by day. They didn't go where they wanted to go.

Some Christians are in a "Catch-22" situation—a real dilemma—because they don't believe that God can reveal His will by the inner witness, the inner voice, dreams, visions and so on. As a result, they can never be sure if it is God's will for them to trust Him for any other miracle except salvation, forgiveness, cleansing from sin, casting out demons and some other **general** Biblical promises. The Bible promises these miracles but doesn't promise that, for example, Mrs Johnson can be assured that if she asks God to give her a job in the solicitor's office, she will get it. There is no Scripture as **specific** as this, which promises someone a **particular** job. Therefore, unless a Christian believes that he can obtain God's will directly from the Holy Spirit about matters like these which the Bible **only generally** covers, he will have to pray an "If it be Thy will" prayer. God will not answer a prayer of "If it be Thy will give me the solicitor's job", or "Lord, open the doors if it be Thy will."[1]

Romans 8:26-27 are verses which show that God the Father wants us to allow His Holy Spirit to show us **how** and

26

what to pray about things about which the Holy Scriptures do not clearly reveal His specific will:

"So too the (Holy) Spirit comes to our aid and bears us up in our weakness; for we do not know WHAT prayer to offer nor HOW to offer it worthily as we ought, but the Spirit Himself goes to meet our supplication and pleads in our behalf with unspeakable yearnings and groanings too deep for utterance. And He Who searches the hearts of men knows what is in the mind of the (Holy) Spirit—what His intent is—because the Spirit intercedes and pleads [before God] in behalf of the saints ACCORDING TO and IN HARMONY WITH GOD'S WILL." (Amplified Version)

A person who really trusts that God loves him, should seek the Holy Spirit's inner guidance about what and how to pray. He should then obey this guidance.

FOOTNOTE:
1. Refer to my booklet "MIRACLES—AND IF IT BE THY WILL" which gives details of the common misinterpretation of Jesus' "If it be Thy will" prayer found in Luke 22:42.

5
Do Miracles Give Authority To One's Teachings?

Many people gullibly do what I used to do. They read a Christian book or hear preaching by someone whom God has used greatly to pray for many healings and other miracles. They then think that because God has used these authors or preachers greatly in praying for miracles, that **everything** or **almost everything** that they write, teach or preach must be what God thinks. Many Protestants have done or still do this today with some of their godly ministries. Many Catholics have done this with some whom they called "Saints", such as Francis of Assisi, Patrick of Ireland, Rita of Cassio, Anthony of Padua, and many others.

An example of this way of thinking is, "St. Francis (or Smith Wigglesworth, or William Branham) was used by God to pray for amazing miracles. He deeply knew God. St. Francis (or Wigglesworth or Branham) taught us to ..... He was so devoted to God, that I'm sure God revealed this to him. People who were as close to God as he was, would not make mistakes about what teachings and practices are inspired by God." Such thinking has led to deception among many churchgoers over the centuries.

They should have checked with God's Scriptures to see if the Lord Jesus, the Apostles, the Prophets and its other God-inspired writers agreed with all the various teachings of Francis of Assisi, any other so-called "Saint", Wigglesworth, Branham and whoever. Remember that every minister, priest or bishop that has ever lived has not understood every part of the teachings of the Scriptures. Every preacher has taught, and every Christian book ever written (except the Bible) contains some things which are not totally in agreement with the way God thinks about the matter. My own books are included in this. Only those parts of what I teach that are 100% in agreement with Scripture are true.

Only the Scriptures are totally God-inspired (see 2 Timothy 3:16, 2 Peter 3:15-17). All other spiritual books are true only in those parts that agree with the teachings of His Scriptures. (Refer to my book "HIGHEST AUTHORITY: CHURCH, SCRIPTURE OR TRADITION?" for more details).

We should all follow the example given in Acts 17:11. The people here checked to see if what the Apostle Paul was teaching was in agreement with the number of Books of the Bible that were available to them at the time. This verse says:

"The people there were more open-minded than the people in Thessalonica. They listened to the message with great earnestness, and EVERY DAY they STUDIED THE SCRIPTURES TO SEE IF WHAT PAUL SAID WAS REALLY TRUE." (Good News Version)

If the Apostle Paul had his teaching checked, **how much more** should we check the teachings of others?

Just because God performs many miracles in the life of a particular television or radio minister, pastor, priest or bishop or pope, this does not mean that everything this ministry is teaching is what God teaches. This is obvious from the fact that many of the men and women for whom God has done many miraculous things, have taught ideas contrary to each other. If everything they all taught was exactly as God thinks, then they would not have taught opposing ideas.

Further proof that having great miracles in a ministry does not mean that everything the person writes or teaches is what God agrees with can be seen in the lives of Alexander Dowie and William Branham, two well-known Pentecostal ministers of yesteryear.

Both Dowie and Branham were used greatly by God in trusting Him for many amazing miracles. But Dowie in the later part of his ministry wrongly taught that he was the fulfilment of the prophecy in Malachi 4:5-6 about the return of Elijah the prophet.

Branham taught some things contrary to Scripture. He taught that before Adam had intercourse with Eve, the serpent had intercourse with her and this produced Cain. Branham then taught all unbelievers since that time were physical descendants of Cain and all believers were descendants of Seth—our fate in heaven or hell being determined by who was our ancestor. Branham taught that the first sin of Eve was having sex with Satan.

Branham also taught that hell is not eternal. He said that sinners and Satan go there only for a time and are then totally annihilated.[1]

MARK 16:20

Some may argue that Mark 16:20 says that often God confirms His Word by miracles. They may then argue that Mark 16:20 infers that if a person has a lot of miracles in his life, this means that everything he is preaching is in agreement with God's Word. But they fail to realize that God only confirms by miracles **those parts** of what the person preaches that are in agreement with His Word. The person may be preaching 80% in agreement with His Word and 20% his own personal religious opinions that he thinks mistakenly are in agreement with His Word. God does not perform miracles to give His seal of authority and approval to the 20% or so personal religious opinion of any Christian man or woman—no matter how great.

God confirms only His Word by miracles. He never performs miracles in a person's life in order to encourage us to believe that everything a particular preacher, evangelist, so-called "Saint", pope, bishop or anyone else has taught or written is without error. Only God's Word is infallible, not that of well-known Christian men or women.

FOOTNOTE:
1. "THE BRANHAM DOCTRINES—A COMPARISON WITH SCRIPTURE", Printed by South Australian A.O.G., Australia, 1971.

6
Prayers Of Presumption

(N.B. Most of this and the next two chapters were written in 1980 to 1981)

Presumption prayer could be defined as trying to use God's miracle-working power in a way that is **not exactly promised** in the Bible or **exactly promised** by the inner guidance of His Holy Spirit. Presumption in prayer is where we expect God to do something for us, even though it **is not His will** for us. Presumption is attempting to believe with our hearts and speak with our mouths that God is going to do a specific miracle for us, even though this miracle **is not His will.**

Presumption involves trying to get God to build **our kingdom,** instead of His Kingdom. As we will see later in this and the next two chapters, presumption can **appear to be true Biblical faith,** even though it is not.

PRESUMPTION INVOLVES SELF-WILL

Presumption is associated with self-will. Self-willed prayers are the opposite of God-willed prayers. The word "presumption" in the Bible means "acting according to our own human will". Deuteronomy 17:12-13, Deuteronomy 18:22 and Psalm 19:13 speak of presumption. Psalm 19:13 says:

"Keep back Your servant also from PRESUMPTUOUS SINS; let them not have dominion over me!"
(Amplified Version)

People who pray with presumption regularly, reveal that they have a very limited understanding of how good is

33

God's will for their lives. If they really knew how good God's will is, they would never ask Him to do things for them that are not His will.

VERSES QUOTED OFTEN

I've read some very godly Christian authors, who unknowingly teach true Biblical faith mixed in with varying degrees of presumption, often quote the following verses to try to prove that their way of praying is 100% Bible-based. These verses are beautiful examples of how God wants us to pray, but they are often interpreted in ways that are contrary to the plain meaning of other verses. John 16:23 says:

"...Truly, truly, I say to you, if you ask anything of the Father, He will give it to you in my name."
(Revised Standard Version)

John 14:14:

"If you ask anything in My name, I will do it."
(Revised Standard Version)

Matthew 21:22:

"And whatever you ask in prayer, you will receive, if you have faith." *(Revised Standard Version)*

Matthew 7:7-8:

"Ask, and it will be given you; seek, and you will find; knock, and it will be opened to you. For everyone who asks receives, and he who seeks finds, and to him who knocks it will be opened."
(Revised Standard Version)

Mark 11:23-24:

"Truly, I say to you, whoever SAYS to this mountain, 'Be taken up and cast into the sea, and DOES NOT DOUBT in his heart, but BELIEVES that what he SAYS will come to pass, it WILL be done for him. Therefore I tell you, whatever you ask in prayer, BELIEVE that you will receive it, and you will."
(Revised Standard Version)

Matthew 18:18:

"Truly, I say to you, whatever you bind on earth shall be bound in heaven, and whatever you loose on earth

shall be loosed in heaven." (Revised Standard Version)

and Matthew 18:19:

> *"Again I say to you, if two of you agree on earth about anything they ask, it will be done for them by my Father in heaven."*   *(Revised Standard Version)*

These are all tremendous verses of Scripture on prayer, but the godly Christian authors[1] who unknowingly and the not-so-godly authors[2] who sometimes knowingly encourage others to pray with varying degrees of presumption tend to take these verses in **isolation** and ignore the truth of other verses of Scripture on prayer, such as James 4:2-3 and Romans 8:26.

We need to note very carefully that the above verses don't tell us **what** we can pray for. These verses tell us **how** we should pray, **after we have found out God's more specific will** from other verses of Scripture and from the inner guidance of the Holy Spirit. By mistakenly not understanding this, many teachers on faith, prayer and miracles have **unknowingly** led many Christians into great disappointment and disillusionment when God has not answered their so-called "faith" request.

Many Christians falsely use these verses as the basis of trying to pray for miracles such as walking on water, getting a particular person to marry them, getting a particular job in exactly the street and town where they would like God to get them a job, and so on.

In general, the Bible promises us that we can get married[3], that God will supply our financial needs and that He will give us His strength, wisdom and help. However, we **cannot** trust God for specific miracles such as walking on water, for rain to come in a time of famine, getting one particular person to marry us and so on unless His Holy Spirit gives us guidance that these **specific** miracles are His will. The Bible doesn't give us **specific** promises for these sorts of things.

A FALSE ARGUMENT

Here is one argument used by some Christian authors that encourages people to pray in presumption: Since 1 John 5:14-15 says that we must ask God according to His will, we can use verses such as John 16:23, John 14:14, Matthew

21:22, Mark 11:23-24 and others listed at the beginning of this chapter as specific indicators of what God wants us to ask Him. The argument reasons, since John 16:23 says, ...*"if you ask anything of the Father, he will give it to you in my name,"* and Matthew 21:22 says, *"....whatever you ask in prayer, you will receive, if you have faith,"* and the other verses say similar things, the Father will give us "anything" or "whatever" we ask if we ask in Jesus' name and we ask in faith.

The above would be a very good argument, except for two things:

- Verses such as John 16:23 and Mark 11:23-24 are not indicators of what God specifically wants us to ask of Him. They are verses which show how God wants us to pray after we have found out specifically what He wants us to ask of Him.
- As we will see later, the words "anything" and "in My name" mean something very different from the meaning taught by those who often unknowingly encourage presumption prayer.

ASKING IN FAITH?

We can't use verses such as John 14:14, Matthew 21:22, Matthew 7:7-8 and Mark 11:23-24 to ask God for anything, even if the thing is not His will. For instance, a man may pray, "Father in the Name of Jesus Christ, I ask that You change me into a woman. I'm standing on Your promise in John 16:23 which says that if I ask anything of the Father in Jesus' Name, He will do it for me. I totally **believe** that You Father are going to make me into a woman. And just as Mark 11:23-24 teaches, I am now **speaking** in faith that You will do as I say. I **do not doubt,** but **believe** that what I am now **speaking** out in faith will come to pass."

This person then speaks in so-called "faith" to every person that he meets, "I believe that the Father is changing me into a woman. I'm standing on the promises of God. And just as Romans 4:17 says, I'm calling those things that are not, as though they already are. Even though I can't see it with my eyes, I believe now that I have received this **from the Father.**"

The person then **acts** in so-called "faith" by buying dresses, bras and other women's clothes, by wearing lipstick, and by making himself look more and more like a woman. In so-called "faith", he changes his name to a woman's name and begins to talk in a high-pitched voice like a woman. He steps out in so-called "faith" and begins to look for a man to marry.

This man is attempting to put into practice many Biblical faith principles, which would be good if what he is specifically asking of God, was God's will. But since he is attempting to believe God for something that is not God's will (see 1 Corinthians 6:9, Romans 1:26-28), his attempt to exercise faith has **no God-inspired foundation** on which to rest. The Lord Jesus would not allow His faith to motivate, inspire and anoint prayer requests such as this man's.

The above man is not specifically asking God **what** God would want him to ask. He would be praying **how** God would want him to pray only if what he was asking for was God's will.[4]

IS GOD OUR SERVANT AND A SPIRITUAL SANTA CLAUS?

Some Christian writers give the wrong conception of God. By using verses such as Matthew 21:21-22 and John 16:23-24 **in ways contrary to the plain meaning of many other verses,** they give the impression that God is like a big spiritual Santa Claus. They seem to suggest that God will give us anything we want as long as we think, visualize and say it long enough.

They emphasize God as being **Our servant** so much that they **underemphasize** that all believers are **His servants.** Christians are sons and daughters of God. But they are **also His servants.** Romans 6:22, Ephesians 6:6 and 1 Peter 2:16 prove this.

Matthew 20:28 does say that Jesus came to serve people. But to suggest that this verse means He will do whatever we ask or desire—even if it is contrary to the Father's will — is an interpretation which is contrary to the plain meaning of many other verses. Matthew 20:28 teaches that Jesus desires to serve or minister to people in ways that a perfectly unselfish king would serve His people—giving to them what **He knows is best, not what they think is best.** The Scriptures say that Jesus is also Our Lord. There are no verses which say that we are Jesus' Lord. Since Jesus is **Lord**, He will choose the ways in which He will serve us.

These authors also seem to suggest that if we desire

37

something, all we have to do is get our thoughts, mental picturing and speaking concentrated on whatever miracles we would like.

They forget that it is impossible for us to have Holy Spirit-inspired faith for a specific miracle unless this miracle is God's will. If the Bible specifically states that the miracle that we want is God's will, or the Holy Spirit through inner guidance tells us that it is God's will, then this Word of the Lord will put God's faith for this miracle in our mind and spirit. Romans 10:17 says:

> *"Faith cometh by hearing, and hearing by the WORD of God."* (Authorised Version)

Once we know God's will about the matter through having a specific Word of the Lord from the Scriptures or from the inner guidance of the Holy Spirit, obviously then the accompanying faith for this miracle that the Holy Spirit puts into our hearts will need to be expressed by—

- **meditating on** the fact that the Person of God the Holy Spirit is definitely performing this miracle,
- **positively saying** that God is doing this miracle for us,
- **not doubting** in our mind that He is doing this miracle for us, and
- **thanking** God that His Spirit is performing this miracle for us.

We will then be doing all of these **actions** of **faith** on the basis that we are sure that the miracle is God's will. If we are not sure that the miracle is God's will, we should not try to exercise faith for His Spirit to perform this miracle for us.

Note also that we have the God-given right to say that the miracle will occur in a **specific way** or at a **specific time,** if He reveals His specific will on these two things.

AN EXAMPLE OF PRESUMPTION

Some of these Christian authors go to ridiculous extremes about positive thinking, positive speaking (also known as positive confession) and correct mental picturing (also called visualizing or dreaming your goals). They suggest that everything (or almost everything) a Christian says, thinks and mentally pictures will result in God doing whatever he is thinking, picturing and saying.

38

For example, one author said that if a Christian keeps believing, saying, thinking and picturing that it is going to rain today, then God's Spirit will then make it rain. How ridiculous! This is making an **idol** of the **human mind** and the **human tongue.** God is not some spiritual Santa Claus up in heaven Who will do everything that a Christian **says, thinks** or **visualizes.**

To show how ridiculous this is, consider what would happen in a city where there are one million Christians, five hundred thousand of whom are thinking and saying that it is going to rain today, and the other five hundred thousand thinking and saying that it is not going to rain today. In this situation, God can't fulfil both groups' positive confessions and so-called "believing", particularly if they live intermingled with each other.

God answered Elijah's prayer for it to rain after three years of drought (see James 5:17-18). But remember that 1 Kings 18:1 says that God the Holy Spirit gave Elijah a Word of the Lord to say that it was His will for Elijah to trust Him to make it rain. Elijah could only think, mentally picture and say that the miracle of it raining would occur because God revealed that it was His will for Elijah to trust Him for this. This is the correct way to pray.

Thinking, mentally picturing and saying that God will perform a miracle for us, is only useful—

1) if the Scripture SPECIFICALLY promises us that this miracle is God's will:

   a) We can think and say with **certainty** that the Lord will give us wisdom when we ask Him for it. This is because James 1:5 **specifically** promises this miracle from God to all people who ask.

   b) We can also think and say with certainty that the Lord will give us His strength to overcome the problems that we face in our lives. This is because Psalm 18:32, 27:1, 46:1, and Jeremiah 16:19 specifically promise that it is God's will that He do these things for us.

2) if God the Holy Spirit gives us inner guidance that the miracle, one not specifically promised in the Scriptures, is His will for us. For example, we are put in prison by a government that hates Christians. Then the Holy Spirit gives us inner guidance after we have been in prison a month that it is the Father's will that we walk

straight through the wall. God will perform this miracle for us, if we exercise faith in Him in our thoughts and words by trusting that this miracle is going to occur and if we obey Him by having our legs take our physical body through the wall at **exactly the time** He tells us He wants us to start going through the wall.

SATAN TEMPTED JESUS TO PRAY IN PRESUMPTION

Another example of presumption is seen in Matthew 4:6-7, where Satan tried to get Jesus to ask God the Father to do a particular thing for Him. In these verses, we see that Satan quoted an Old Testament promise that God would send His angels to protect a believer who was in danger of being hurt (see Psalm 91:11-12).

In this historical event, we see that Satan tried to get Jesus to use this promise in a way that was **not exactly** promised in the Old Testament. This promise spoke of people being given protection when they came into danger **accidentally.** But Satan tried to get Jesus to **deliberately** jump off the Temple and then expect God the Father to send angels to protect Him. Jesus resisted this temptation to use God the Father's miracle-working power for "showing off purposes," or for "personal excitement purposes", or other similar wrong purposes which were **not exactly promised** in Scripture.

PRESUMPTION OF TWO DISCIPLES

Another example of people praying in presumption is seen in Luke 9:53-56. Here, the disciples James and John wanted to use God's power in a way that was **not exactly promised** in the Scriptures, nor was promised to them by the Holy Spirit. These two disciples wanted to use His power to kill some people who had offended and hurt them.

The disciples may have wrongly thought since the Lord Jesus said in John 14:14, *"If you ask ANYTHING in my name, I will do it"* (Revised Standard Version), and in Mark 11:23, *"Whosoever SAYS to this mountain, 'Be taken up and cast into the sea', and DOES NOT DOUBT in his heart, but believes that what he says will come to pass, it will be done for him"* (Revised Standard Version), that God the Father would certainly answer any prayer request by them for the miraculous killing of those who had hurt them. Would some Christians in the same circumstances today very possibly ask God for the same thing on the basis of these Scriptures?

God in Christ refused to answer this prayer, because what the disciples were asking for in so-called "faith" was not the Father's will. Their "faith" for this miracle was not Bible-based Holy Spirit-inspired faith. It was merely a human fleshly effort to exercise faith for this miracle. This example provides a good lesson for us.

Many Christian writers who mistakenly teach about faith in ways that lead others into presumption are devoted, born-again Christians. It is just that they interpret some verses or passages of Scripture in ways that disagree with the meaning of other verses or passages. They **quote certain verses** and **passages constantly,** giving the appearance that all they are saying is supported by Scripture. But they ignore other verses and passages such as those quoted here. To avoid such imbalance, they need to consider **as a whole** all of the verses and passages which talk of trusting God for miracles.

ANOTHER PRESUMPTION OF JAMES AND JOHN

One of the clearest examples in the Holy Scriptures of presumption is found in Mark 10:35-45, again with the Apostles James and John. Verses 35 to 37 say:

"And James and John, the sons of Zebedee, approached Him, and said to Him, Teacher we DESIRE You to do for us WHATEVER we ASK of You. And He replied to them, What do you DESIRE Me to do for you? And they said to Him, Grant that we may sit one at Your right hand and one at (Your) left hand, in Your glory—Your majesty and splendor."
(Amplified Version)

The Lord Jesus said to them in the above a similar thing that He said to the leper (see Mark 10:51): *"What do you desire Me to do for you?"*

Hundreds of other people had asked Jesus to do other things for them and He did as they asked. Blind people asked Him to make them see and He did (see Matthew 9:27-29, Mark 10:46-52). People with dreaded leprosy asked Him to heal them and He did (see Matthew 8:1-4,

41

Luke 17:11-19). Jesus healed the servant of a Roman centurion who asked (see Matthew 8:5-13). He cast out a demon from a young girl when her mother asked Him (see Matthew 15:21-28) and out of an epileptic because his father asked (see Matthew 17:14-18).

But in this instance, the Lord Jesus refused to do what the two disciples asked. How could this be the case though, if the Scripture, *"If you ask anything in My name, I will do it"* (John 14:14, Revised Standard Version), and similar frequently quoted verses mean that God will give us anything we ask if we add the words "in Jesus' Name" on the end of our request, even if what we ask is not His will?

Jesus' answer to them is seen in verse 38:

"But Jesus said to them, YOU DO NOT KNOW WHAT YOU ARE ASKING. Are you able to drink the cup that I drink, or be baptized with the baptism (of affliction) with which I am baptized?"
                                            (Amplified Version)

Some might foolishly say that James and John were not believing and confessing positively enough. But nowhere in this example, does the Lord Jesus tell them that this was their problem. He told others when their problem in not receiving was a lack of faith—Peter (see Matthew 14:22-31) and the disciples who could not cast the demon out of the epileptic boy (see Matthew 17:14-20).

The Lord told James and John that their problem in this circumstance was that they were **not asking according to God's will.** Jesus' words in verse 40 reveal this:

"But to sit at My right hand or at My left hand is not Mine to give; but (will be given those) for whom it is ORDAINED and PREPARED." *(Amplified Version)*

The Lord was not going to try to change the Father's will, just because two puny Apostles asked Him to.

James and John had begun their conversation with the Lord Jesus about the matter with almost the same words as the Scripture, *"If you ask anything in My name, I will do it"* (John 14:14). They said, *"....Teacher, we DESIRE You to do for us WHATEVER we ASK OF YOU."* (Mark 10:35, Amplified Version).

But the Lord Jesus answered them with words that should shock those who believe that God will give us anything that we desire or ask even if it is not according to His will. Jesus said to them, "YOU DO NOT KNOW WHAT YOU ARE ASKING..."

Only a **short time after** this, when they went to Jerusalem, Jesus said to them the words found in the the oft-quoted verses Mark 11:23-24. These verses say that if we ask God for something, believe in our hearts and confess with our mouths that He will do it for us, He will. But since just previously in the case of James' and John's request, Jesus had shown that we should only ask for things that are God the Father's will, the principles of Mark 11:23-24 only result in a miracle, when we are asking for what He wants us to ask.

To all of us who are praying in presumption, Jesus would probably say, "You DO NOT KNOW WHAT YOU ARE ASKING..." Jesus would probably say to us, "You think what you are asking is best for you, but with My infinite knowledge, I know it is not good for you. If I answered your request, this would be **a lack of love** for you on my part."

As the Lord stated in verse 38, if God were to answer all our prayer requests, other consequences might occur, consequences which we **never expected.** A barren wife might ask God to enable her to become pregnant this month. But God might know that this woman's mother and father are going to die in a few months and that this woman will be emotionally unwell for a long period. God might foresee that if she was pregnant then, the baby would be emotionally scarred. The woman would be unaware of these consequences of her request. God might prefer to enable her to become pregnant at a future time.

AN APPROPRIATE COMMENT

As a good minister whom I know emphasised, "Presumption can result, for example, in a Christian parent who can't even run his/her family properly, thinking that he/she can tell Our all-knowing, all-powerful, totally loving God how He should run the Universe."

FOOTNOTES:
   1. I will not name these authors because I am not attacking them but some of the ideas they teach.

Prayers Of Presumption

2. Not all Christian authors who are caught in the presumption trap are very godly. Some of them make outlandish promises to their readers that God will give them every or almost every selfish desire and whim their readers have. These authors do this in order to gain popularity and/or get big money collections at the end of their preaching engagements or for similar selfish reasons.

3. This is unless we are among the very small number of people God calls to a ministry that requires us to be single (see Matthew 19:11-12). The Apostle Paul is an example of this.

4. If you have been involved in the sin of homosexuality, or have been a practicing transvestite (a person who wants to be the opposite sex to how God created him/her), do not think that I'm saying that you cannot trust God to restore you to the way that He intended. He never desired for you to be a homosexual or transvestite.

7
Presumption Or Faith?

The following is an example of Christians thinking that they were exercising faith. This incident resulted in **terrible failure.**

STEPPING OUT IN SO-CALLED "FAITH"

In South Korea a few years ago, there were some tremendous Christian youth meetings on Samgak Mountain. Many young people flocked to the meetings. During the week of the youth campaign, rain fell very heavily. As a result, all of the rivers overflowed. A group of young people desired to cross one river in order to get to the meetings on the other side. There was no bridge or boat for miles.

Three girls tried to exercise faith in the wrong way that many Christians do these days. They said, "Why can't we just wade through the water? Peter walked on the water, and Peter's God is our God, Peter's Jesus is our Jesus, and Peter's faith is our faith. Peter believed and we should do all the more. We are going to go over this river!" Some Christians on reading this would say that these girls were exercising tremendous faith by speaking and acting the way that they did.

These girls then knelt down and held hands together, quoting the Scriptures containing the story of Peter walking on the water. They claimed to believe just as Peter did, and began to wade through the water. Tragically, they were swept away by the flood and three days later, their bodies were found in the open sea.

Non-Christian newspapers attacked the churches because of this so-called "faith". The headlines "Their God Could Not Save Them" and "Why Did God Not Answer Their Prayer of Faith?" are two examples. Many good Christians throughout Korea lost their faith as a result of this incident. These backsliders thought to themselves, "These girls believed exactly as our ministers have taught; they exercised their faith. From the platform, our ministers constantly urge the people to boldly exercise their faith in the Word of God. These girls did just that, so why didn't God answer? Our God must not be a living God."

Have you had a similar sort of experience to these girls? The reason these girls drowned was that nowhere in the Bible does God specifically promise that anyone can walk on water. He has specifically promised in the Bible that we can be saved (see Romans 10:9, John 3:16-18) and we can have the Holy Spirit and His presence and power in us (see Luke 11:13, Acts 1:8). The Bible also promises that God has given to every born-again Christian the authority and power to cast out demons (see Luke 10:17-19, Mark 9:38-40, 16:17, Ephesians 6:12-18, James 4:7)[1] and that God will give us His strength (see Psalm 28:7, Philippians 2:13, 4:13) and His wisdom (see James 1:5, John 14:26) that we need to live according to His will.

However, we can't find a specific promise which says that God promises Christians who want to walk on water that they will be able to.

The Bible does have some general promises such as Mark 11:23-24, Matthew 18:18-20 and John 14:14, which could cover instances of walking on water if God willed us to do this. However, there is **no blank cheque given** in these verses of Scripture which could prove that it was God's will for all Christians to walk on water at any time they may wish to.

Mark 11:23-24, Matthew 18:18-20 and John 14:14, if taken by themselves, could be falsely taken to mean that we could ask for anything, even if the "anything" was outside God's will, and He would give it to us.

For example, the word "anything" includes praying for all the world's wealth, praying for the next-door neighbour's husband to leave his wife and marry you, praying that God will kill our enemy, praying that He will give a drug addict millions of dollars worth of drugs, praying that He will give an alcoholic a wine company and so on. Obviously, these prayers are **against God's will** as shown in the rest of the Bible. Therefore, we can think and speak in so-called "faith", resist doubt and act as though we will get an answer

46

to these prayer requests, but they will NEVER be answered.

The word "anything" in verses such as John 14:14 must be **cross-referenced** with **John 15:7** and **1 John 5:14** to see what the "anything" really means. John 15:7 says:

*"If you live in Me—abide vitally united to Me—and MY WORDS remain in you and continue to live in your hearts, ask **whatever you will** and it shall be done for you."*   *(Amplified Version)*

1 John 5:14 says:

"And this is the confidence—the assurance, the (privilege of) boldness—which we have in Him: (we are sure) that if we ask ANYTHING (make any request) ACCORDING TO HIS WILL... He listens to and hears us."   *(Amplified Version)*

Here in these Scriptures, the **"Whatever you will"** and **"anything"** are **linked** to God's will.

Positive confession, resisting doubt, thinking and acting as though God has already given us the answer, will only work **if** our prayer request is based on a **specific unambiguous promise** in Scripture or **if God the Holy Spirit** speaks a **Word of the Lord** to us to reveal the Father's will.

The girls who drowned in Korea failed to realise that the verses of Scripture they quoted about Peter **didn't apply to them.** In the incident of Peter walking on water, the Lord Jesus told Peter that it was **His will** for Peter to walk on the water (see Matthew 14:22-32). Jesus spoke a Word of the Lord in Matthew 14:29 to Peter telling him on that **specific occasion** that it was God's will for him to exercise faith to be able to walk on water. Jesus said, "Come." Peter **didn't act in presumption.** This is why the Lord gave Peter the power to walk on water. It was when Peter started doubting the Word of the Lord that he began to sink.

The only way that those Korean girls could have walked on water would have been if the Lord Jesus, through the Person of God the Holy Spirit, had revealed to them that the Father willed for them to miraculously walk on water. However, Jesus didn't say "Come" to them. They acted in presumption, thinking that they were exercising faith and, like the Israelites in Numbers 14:40-45, there was terrible failure. Deuteronomy 1:43 speaks of this same sin of **mis-**

47

taking presumption for **faith.**

PSEUDO-FAITH

The three Korean girls acted in presumption, in a way that APPEARED to be faith. They were presumptuous by disobeying God. They disobeyed God by expecting this miracle without a Word of the Lord.

They had what can be called **pseudo-faith.** The word "pseudo" means "**seeming** to be something, but not really being it". Pseudo-faith is a purely **man-made** attempt to trust God for some miracle—one which He has never revealed specifically from His Scriptures, or through the inner guidance of His Holy Spirit is His will.

Pseudo-faith is **fleshly** and involves trying to get God's assistance **in building "our little kingdoms".** It does not involve building God's Kingdom, even though those who pray with pseudo-faith often mistakenly claim that they are building His Kingdom. Sometimes, what people call "stepping out in faith" is really pseudo-faith.

The Bible in John 8:47 says:

"Whoever is of God listens to God.—Those who belong to God HEAR the WORDS OF GOD."
(Amplified Version)

This means that a true Christian listens to **all of the Bible** which is the written Word of God. It also means that a true Christian listens to the Words of the Lord that God the Holy Spirit frequently speaks to us.

However, these Holy Spirit revelations will **never** tell us to do things contrary to the teachings of the Scriptures. For example, if you have an impression deep within your mind that God wants you to marry the Pastor's wife and kill the Pastor, realise that this is not a revelation from the Holy Spirit. The Holy Spirit is the author of the Bible. He wouldn't contradict Himself. He said in the Bible adultery and murder are against the Father's will.

The Lord Jesus in John 10:27 promises to speak to Christians. He said:

"The sheep that are My own HEAR and ARE LISTENING TO MY VOICE, and I know them and they follow Me."　　　*(Amplified Version)*

MARRIAGE

Some people on the basis of the Scripture Mark 11:23, which they believe means in paraphrased form, *"You can have what you say"*, **presumptuously** choose a specific person and claim this person in prayer as their husband or wife. It is true that God promises nearly everyone a husband or wife (see Hebrews 13:4 and 1 Corinthians 7:2), but we cannot in presumption choose which person specifically.

We must let God reveal to us whom He wants us to marry. We should not let ourselves become seriously emotionally involved with a member of the opposite sex, unless God has clearly revealed that this is His will. Also, we have no God-given right to choose at what time He will provide a husband or wife. We should **trust** that **He knows the right time.**

DELAYING JESUS' SECOND COMING?

Consider the following situation: You are 25 years old. You desire to live to 80 years of age, so you begin to speak out in so-called "faith" telling your family, friends and others that God is going to ensure that you live another 55 years. You quote to them Mark 11:23-24, John 14:14 and similar oft-quoted verses. You think that you are believing with your heart and speaking with your mouth the way these verses indicate.

However, what if God the Father's perfect will is for Jesus Christ to return to Earth in eight years from now in order to set up His Kingdom? Do you think the Father will change His wonderful plans about the Second Coming of Jesus Christ— these plans affecting the welfare of millions and millions of other people—just to fit in with your **selfish little** so-called "goal of faith".

If you answer "No" to this last question, you are proving to yourself that verses such as Mark 11:23-24, Matthew 21:22, John 14:14 and so on, only refer to situations in which what you are asking is God's will.

If you instead answer "Yes" to this last question, you are revealing to yourself that your understanding of "faith" in some areas is not really in agreement with God's written Word.

If God was to answer such requests, the Second Coming of Jesus Christ could be delayed forever, by just one person in each generation "believing" and "confessing" that the

Father will allow them to live to 80 years of age.

The above comments do not mean that if God gave you a revelation it was His will for you to live to 80 years of age, that you should not then in true God-inspired faith believe Him to bring this about. He would only inspire you to believe Him for this, if it was not His will for the Lord Jesus to return to Earth before this.

MANY TELEVISION MINISTRIES AND WELL-KNOWN PREACHERS IN THE U.S.

Many of the most popular Pentecostal and Charismatic television preachers at the present time **in the United States** have fallen into this error. **Part** of what many of these preachers teach is **true Biblical faith,** but **another part** is based on **presumption.** Some other well-known American preachers have fallen into the same error.

These television ministries and well-known preachers are **probably unaware** that part of what they are teaching is presumption. Many of them in previous years probably heard preaching or read books which seemed to present good reasons for accepting the false interpretations of John 14:14, John 16:23 and similar oft-quoted verses. Unknowingly, these preachers then began to preach similarly.

Thankfully, some American television preachers have not fallen into this error.

The First Group

One group of these American preachers in their books or when speaking **mention in passing** that our dreams or goals or prayer requests must be God-inspired. They **do not emphasize this crucial point much.** Nor in detail do they say how God reveals His will by His Holy Spirit about things not revealed specifically in His Scriptures. (How they ever think that we can have God-inspired goals or dreams without teaching people clearly how to recognize the guidance of the Holy Spirit, I find remarkable!) As a result, many Christian listeners or readers race away and start visualizing, confessing and "believing" for their own so-called "faith" goals and dreams that were never inspired by God in the first place. Many times, I've seen this happen.

At present, the above lack of emphasis on the importance of always seeking God's desires and will about matters which the Scriptures do not reveal God's specific will, also is causing many Christians to become self-reliant—often without them realizing this. It is also resulting in many believers having little devotion to seeking daily the guidance of the Holy Spirit and having little desire to obey God's command for them to be His vessels—being available for whatever use or purpose He (not we) regard as best.

Even though some of these preachers talk much about faith and being filled daily with the Holy Spirit, some (but obviously not all) of what they preach encourages the reverse. Instead of causing Christians to be controlled by the Holy Spirit and to walk in true Biblical faith—trust, dependence and reliance on God and the seeking of His will and desires instead of our own—unknowingly, they are encouraging Christians to be controlled by many of their own desires and will. They are under-emphasizing the strong Biblical teaching on growing in holiness (Refer to my book "KEYS TO KNOWING GOD BETTER" to see what holiness is). This is helping to produce many "wishy-washy," lukewarm, weak believers especially in the United States and other Western countries. God wishes to give great blessings to His people. But these lukewarm believers are more interested in obtaining His blessings than in loving, intimately knowing, obeying and depending on Him. They love Him to a certain degree. But they love **what they can get from Him** far more.

Some belonging to this particular group of preachers use such words as "success" constantly in their preaching or books. The Scriptures use the word "success" in Joshua 1:7-8. But as we can see in these verses, God uses the word "success" as being simply the fulfilling of His will as is revealed in His Scriptures. Verses such as James 2:20-23, Galatians 5:16 and John 10:27 reveal that in God's eyes, success is also obedience to His Holy Spirit's guidance.

This particular group teaches that we must obey the Scriptures to be a successful Christian. But because they underemphasize or neglect to emphasize the importance of the Holy Spirit's guidance in determining whether a believer's goals or dreams are the Father's will and because they teach little or nothing about how to recognize His guidance, they lead many believers into a great misconception. This false idea is that the Bible defines "successful Christians" as those who obey only the general teachings of the Bible itself, but about matters which the Bible does not give specific guidance on, decide themselves what goals or desires they wish to have.

These preachers do not emphasize that many unbelievers achieve "success" in obtaining goals or dreams or desires that are not God's will for their lives. So just because a Christian achieves "success" by seeing the fulfillment of some goal or dream he had, by positively confessing, visualizing and seemingly "believing" God that this goal or dream will occur, does not mean that He brought this about miraculously. It may have been a purely natural occurrence of some goal contrary to the Holy Spirit's will.

The Second Group

Another group of these well-known preachers teach much about the guidance of the Holy Spirit. They have a very good understanding of how the Holy Spirit speaks. I have greatly appreciated other things I've read in their books or heard them say. But sadly, some of these godly preachers do not emphasize continually the enormous importance for us of checking with the Holy Spirit to see whether our so-called "faith" goals or desires or dreams (about matters which the Scriptures do not reveal God's specific will) are really His will for us. I will not name these preachers. This is because I am not attacking individuals in this book. I aim only to attack false or partially true teachings.

The Third Group

Then there is a third group of preachers who encourage presumption. These are very carnal, fleshly and know little of growing in holiness. They use Biblical words such as "faith", "believing", "God's will" and so on to justify their own and others' selfishness. They are born-again and claim often to be greatly anointed by the Holy Spirit. They boast sometimes of their so-called "great faith".

Purely out of His love and mercy, God sometimes performs miracles for those who come to listen to these preachers. God works miraculously in such meetings **in spite of** the preacher, not because of any great commitment to God or faith on his part.

MANY ARE GODLY PEOPLE

Many of the preachers, who teach about faith in a way that results in their listeners or readers praying in presumption, are **godly people.** It is just that over the years, they have accepted **a common misinterpretation** of such verses as John 16:23, John 14:14, Matthew 21:22 and Mark 11:23-24.

Some of these preachers are exceptionally devoted to God. But a high level of devotion does not guarantee that their teachings will be without error.

I'm hoping that many of these American television preachers and others are humble enough to admit their mistake. This is especially since they have influenced so many Christians in the U.S. and other countries. All preachers need to be wholly concerned with glorifying God instead of themselves, teaching in agreement with the teachings of the Scriptures as much as possible and helping those whom they teach know and love God more than ever. If they have written books and preached thousands of sermons which unknowingly led people to pray in presumption, they need to humbly admit their mistake. **Whatever the cost** in terms of reputation as a "great" preacher or money earned from the sale of their books or tapes, they **must be loyal first to God.** They must learn to be like St. Augustine of Hippo. In his later years, he wrote saying how some of his earlier writings and preaching had been wrong.

CONCLUDING COMMENTS

If a prayer request is based on the Word of the Lord from the Scriptures or from the Holy Spirit, it will be **certainly** answered, if faith is exercised. However, presumption prayers are examples of totally wasted energy and breath in 99% of cases. Many good Christian books on faith don't explain that presumption prayers are bad.

Many people try to **move ahead of God,** just as Paul did, in his enthusiasm to bring the Gospel to others (see Acts 16:6-7).

Presumption is a **fleshly counterfeit** of true Biblical faith. Sadly, it has caught too many Christians in its tangled web.

FOOTNOTE:
1. Born-again Christians may not know how to be a vessel of God's power and authority in the casting out of demons. But this does not change the fact that God has given them His power and authority to do so.

8
Presumption Or
God's Will?

Our responsibility, under **the direction of the Holy Spirit,** is to discover the things for which God the Father is requiring faith from each one of us personally. Then we should set ourselves to believe for **those things** and **no others.** If we seek to exercise faith for anything which lies outside of God's purpose for our lives, this is to step from faith into **presumption.** This is a certain way to ruin part of our lives.

The Scriptures encourage us to ask God for things (see Matthew 7:7-8). For example, it is not wrong to ask God whether you can marry a specific man— say called John— whom you know. But after asking, you must be willing to wait until the Holy Spirit shows you whether it is the Father's will for you to marry John. You cannot try to trust God to bring about a marriage to John unless He shows you it is His will. To try to trust Him to do so without a revelation of His will is not Biblical faith, but presumption.

Many of us need to learn that if we ask God to do some specific thing, we cannot expect Him to do it unless He shows us that our request is His will.

We can pray for a million years and think that we are exercising faith for a particular answer, but unless the particular answer that we are seeking is in line with God's will, our prayer request **will never be answered by Him in 99% of cases.** (Refer to "Asking Outside Of God's Will" chapter for details on the few exceptions).

Before expecting God to perform a miracle, you should find out what is His will about the matter. God's will is found mainly by two means:

First, look for promises in the Bible. For example, if

you want love in your heart towards other people, look for Scriptures which relate to God's willingness to pour His love into your heart. If you want to be born again, receive the Lord Jesus Christ and the Person of God the Holy Spirit into your heart, refer to the Promise of God in Romans 10:9:

> *"Because if you acknowledge and confess with your lips that Jesus is Lord and in your heart believe (adhere to, trust in and rely on the truth) that God raised Him from the dead, you will be saved." (Amplified Version)*

If you lack wisdom, find such verses as James 1:5 and John 14:26 which promise that God will teach you His truth and give you wisdom about any spiritual, emotional, mental, family and other problems that you may have.

If the Bible already shows what His will is about a certain matter, don't pray asking Him to show you His will by some other means. For example, don't ask God whether it is His will for you to marry an unbeliever, for the Bible already gives the answer (see 2 Corinthians 6:14).

Secondly, ask God the Holy Spirit to reveal the Father's will to you by **inner witnesses** and **inner voices of the Holy Spirit and other means.**

PRAYING TO BE A MILLIONAIRE

We should not be fooled as are some Christians. They believe that just because the Bible promises us that God will provide our needs (see Philippians 4:19), we can use this as a promise to become a millionaire. The Bible merely states that God wants to give material blessings to a Christian. The Bible does not state how much God wants to give an individual Christian. God's will for an individual Christian may be very different from what it is for another. God may want to make one Christian a millionaire so he can help missionaries, but He may not wish to make another Christian in the same local church a millionaire.

Our duty is to **constantly prayerfully seek to know God's will.** Then we should exercise this God-inspired faith that what He tells us is His will for us will come to pass. If God tells us that it is His will for us to be a millionaire, and then we don't trust Him to do this for us, we are sinning.

However, if God doesn't show us that it is His will for us to be a millionaire, and we constantly pray that He does make us a millionaire, we are sinning because we are lusting after money and are out of God's will. Our prayer should be "Not my will, but Yours be done" (see Matthew 26:39), just as the Lord Jesus prayed.

AN EXAMPLE FROM EXODUS

An example of the exercise of God-inspired faith is in Exodus Chapter 7. In these verses, we can see that Moses didn't step out in presumption and begin to try to trust God to perform miracles without having first had God tell him God's will about the matter. Moses acted in obedience to God's will. **First, he found God's will** (see Exodus 7:1-9). God revealed to Moses what He wanted Moses to have faith about. Then Moses acted in **faith** and **obedience** to **God's revealed will** (see Exodus 7:10). Moses, when performing a miracle, did it in God-inspired faith. In later chapters, we will study Moses in more detail.

ASK FOR ANYTHING IN MY NAME

I have known of people to backslide because they wrongly interpret the Scripture, *"If you ask Me for anything in My name, I will do it"* (John 14:4, Good News Version), to mean that they can make God into a sort of big spiritual Santa Claus who will give them anything that they desire or any goal they visualize.

This Scripture really means, "You may ask me anything ACCORDING TO MY WILL and I will do it". Proof of this is that in Bible times, the Hebrews attached far more significance to what a person's name was than what many nationalities do these days. Today, names are mostly only used to distinguish one person from another. But the Hebrews regarded the name of a person also as being intimately related to the **character** and **desires** of the same person.[1] A man was called Nabal—the Hebrew word for fool—to describe his character (see 1 Samuel 25:25). God changed the names of Abram (meaning "exalted father") to Abraham (meaning "father of a multitude") (see Genesis 17:5), Sarai (meaning possibly "contentious") to Sarah (meaning "princess") (see Genesis 17:15), Jacob (meaning "He supplants" or "the supplanter") to Israel (meaning "He strives with God" or "God strives") (see Genesis 35:9-12), Simon (meaning "hearing") to Peter (meaning "a piece of rock") (see John 1:42) to describe changes in their **characters** or changes **in**

God's will for their lives.

When God told Adam to give names to the animals, birds and every other living creature, He was telling Adam to do far more than give them words which would distinguish them from each other. God wanted Adam to, under the anointing of the Holy Spirit, describe what the **character** and **desires** of each type of animal, bird and so on would be.

This same principle is seen in Acts 26:9:

"I myself was convinced that I ought to do many things in opposing the name of Jesus of Nazareth."
(Revised Standard Version)

To oppose the "Name" of Jesus Christ, to the author of Acts, was the same as opposing the **Person** of Jesus Christ Himself. To oppose the Person of Jesus Christ meant opposing His **character, teachings** and **His will** about everything.

This is why to pray in the Name of Jesus Christ means **far more** than just attaching the words "in the Name of Jesus" to the end of each of our prayer requests for miracles. It means also to ask for things that would be **in agreement with His will.** It means desiring the Father to only do things for us that Jesus Christ would desire to do for us. In our prayer requests, it is correct using the words "in the Name of Jesus Christ." But remember that to wholly pray in Jesus' Name is to pray also according to His will and desires.

If we are not praying according to God's will, desires and goals—but according to our will, desires and goals—we may think we are praying in Jesus' name, but we are not. In God's eyes, we are praying only **in our own name**. Many are totally unaware of this.

Remember that Bible verses cannot be taken in isolation. They must **be studied in relation to other Bible verses.** 1 John 5:14-15 must be combined with John 14:14 before we can understand what John 14:14 really means. 1 John 5:14-15 says:

"And this is the confidence—the ASSURANCE, the [privilege of] boldness—which we have in Him: [we are SURE] that if we ask ANYTHING (make any request) ACCORDING TO HIS WILL (in agreement with HIS OWN PLAN) He listens to and hears us. And if (since) we [positively] know that He listens to us in whatever we ask, we also know [with SETTLED

*and ABSOLUTE knowledge] that we have [granted us
as our present possessions] the requests made of Him."
(Amplified Version)*

1 John 5:14 says that our prayer requests must match God's plan. Prayer requests based on our own plans which are not in line with His plan, will not be answered in 99% of cases. If we have a **goal** or **dream** to be rich or to travel to Asia or Europe, be a great sportsman, or start a new business and so on, and our goal is **not based on God's plan or will,** we can forget about asking God to help us. 1 John 5:15 says that once we ask according to God's will, we can be **absolutely sure** that God will answer. This is how the Scriptures tell us to ask of God.

God's will is revealed by the written words of the Bible or by His Holy Spirit speaking deep within our mind and spirit. If our goal or plan is not based on God's will, the Lord Jesus will not give us His faith (see Galatians 2:20) to believe that the Father will answer our request. Without the Lord Jesus giving us His faith to be sure that the Father will answer our request, we will only be exercising fleshly, merely man-inspired pseudo-faith. Romans 10:17 says that faith comes by hearing the Word of God. If our prayer is based on **our own fleshly goal or plan** or **our own human will,** we will only be exercising **positive thinking devoid of Holy Spirit-inspired faith.**

It is true that once we are born again, we have the Lord Jesus' faith within us. But He will not allow this faith to be exercised for purposes other than God the Father's will. Some wrongly think that Jesus' faith within them can be used even for things contrary to the Father's will.

THE SEVEN SONS OF SCEVA

The Bible tells us to pray in the Name of Jesus (see John 14:14, John 16:23). However, I've heard some Christians try to use the Name of Jesus as though it is a **magical formula** that can be added on to the end of their prayer requests to ensure their specific desires or goals will be granted by God—desires which could not be His will.

I've seen others who have tried to use the Name of Jesus like a **pagan chant.** They thought that God would move by His power to do things they desired, even though these were not His will, if they kept repeating the word "Jesus" or the

59

words "in the Name of the Lord Jesus" over and over again. They are very similar to the seven sons of Sceva, spoken of in Acts 19:13-16:

> *"Some Jews who traveled around and drove out evil spirits also TRIED TO USE THE NAME OF THE LORD JESUS to do this. They said to the evil spirits, 'I command you in the name of Jesus, whom Paul preaches.' Seven brothers, who were sons of a Jewish High Priest named Sceva, were doing this. But the evil spirit said to them, 'I know Jesus, and I know about Paul; but you—who are you?' The man who had the evil spirit in him attacked them with such violence that he overpowered them all. They ran away from his house, wounded and with their clothes torn off."*
> *(Good News Version)*

It is God's will that demons be cast out of some people (see Mark 16:17). But the Bible nowhere teaches that it is His will that people who are not His born-again sons or daughters will be given His power to cast these demons out. So the seven sons of Sceva had no God-given right to use the Name of the Lord Jesus in this way.

Even born-again Christians have no God-given right to try to use the Name of Jesus for anything that is not the Father's will.

ANOTHER FALSE INTERPRETATION
Many people quote Psalm 37:4:

> *"Delight thyself also in the Lord; and He shall give thee the desires of thine heart."* *(Authorised Version)*

They take this verse to mean that if they are committed to loving God and to praising and worshipping Him, then this will result in God becoming willing to give them whatever desire or goal they have, even if their desire is against His will. They seem to think that God will change His plans for them, as long as they achieve what seems to be a devotion and love for God.

They are wrong in that they interpret this verse contrary to the plain teachings of many other verses of Scripture. They pluck out verses such as Psalm 37:4 and try to make them say things contrary to other verses, such as Matthew 6:33:

"But seek ye FIRST the Kingdom of God, and his righteousness; and all these things shall be added unto you."   *(Authorised Version)*

The Kingdom of God relates to God's rule in heaven and the spiritual world (see 2 Timothy 4:18), but it also relates to His rule over our **human spirit, mind** and **body** (see Luke 17:20-21) and over the **daily activities** of our lives (see Matthew 7:21). For God to rule us in this way, would mean that He would have **to rule over whatever desires** our heart would have. If we do not let God rule and develop whatever our desires may be, **He is not King** of every part of us. We are **our own king in many areas.**

If we think that a desire that we have which is not according to His will would be better for us than the desires that He would like us to have, this shows that we **doubt His wisdom.** We don't really believe that He totally loves us and is working for our best.

1 Corinthians 10:31 says:

"So then, whether you eat or drink, or WHATEVER YOU MAY DO, do ALL for the honour and glory of God."   *(Amplified Version)*

As stated previously in the Introduction, doing everything for the glory of God means thinking, speaking and doing **everything** in our lives in a way that **honours God above everyone** and **everything else.** If our desires for food, houses, sex in marriage, friendship, children, love, a job, and so on are based on the motivation of doing and having these things in a way that somehow honours God and is according to His revealed will in our lives, they are for God's glory. For example, if we desire children and our desire is centred on such things as wishing to teach them to know and love God and to unselfishly love others and to obey His will in all spiritual and natural things, then this desire is for the glory of God.

If our desire for sex in marriage is centred on such desires as wishing to express God's love to the person we are married to—making them feel that we totally accept them with all of their faults and failings just as He does—and is done in such a caring unselfish way that we would not feel ashamed if the Lord Jesus were standing in the room, this is for God's glory.

If our desires are not based on in some way bringing God glory, we cannot use Psalm 37:4 as a means of trying to force Him to give us them.

If we take Psalm 37:4 in relation to verses such as Matthew 6:33 and 1 Corinthians 10:31, we see that it has a different meaning from what some give it. Similarly, God would not say in another Scripture that some of our desires can be evil (see Psalm 10:3), if He meant by Psalm 37:4 that He would give us desires that are not His will.

The people who misinterpret Psalm 37:4 in the above way are also suggesting that we can "earn" answers from God by being a dedicated Christian. We cannot earn anything from God (see Ephesians 2:4-9, Titus 3:3-6).

Psalm 37:4 really means that if we delight ourselves in God—love Him deeply, rely on Him more and more and aim to allow Him to control more and more of our mind, emotions and body, we will come more and more to wish to see **what God desires** occur here on Earth. This will then result in the desires of our hearts becoming more and more in agreement to His desires. Then as we aim to see His desires occur in our lives, He will give us these desires.

He will give us our desires, **because they are really His wonderful desires.**

DREAMING DREAMS

On one American Christian television programme and in a number of Christian books, I've observed a teaching which emphasizes the dreaming of dreams in the exercising of faith. This teaching claims to be Bible-based by the fact that many times in the Scriptures, we observe that individuals were given dreams by God—dreams which they trusted God to fulfil (see Matthew 2:12, 2:22, Genesis 37:5-11, Daniel 7:1-28).

The main weakness of this teaching is it does not emphasize that **in English** the word "dream" **has a number of meanings.** The word "dream" can refer to God revealing His will by **supernaturally** speaking words or putting a mental picture into the sleeping person's mind. The word "dream" also refers to **mere human goals** and **plans.**[2] By not showing the difference between the two, this teaching encourages many to pray in presumption—thinking their mere human goals are the same as the dreams God supernaturally gave to people such as Jacob, Joseph and Daniel.

THE GOD-KIND OF FAITH

I've read a number of Christian books which talk about what they call "the God-kind of faith." The authors of these books use Mark 11:22-24 as the supposed Scriptural foundation of this teaching.

The authors of these books—some of whom are godly men—rightly suggest that sometimes faith is partially expressed by speaking out what we are trusting God to do. They give proof of this by saying that when God created the Universe, He spoke it into being in faith.

But the major weakness of these books is they don't explain that another necessary aspect of what could be called "the God-kind of faith" is asking and trusting God only for those miracles that are **specifically promised** in His Scriptures or by the guidance of the Holy Spirit. By neglecting to explain this clearly, many of these authors are indirectly encouraging their readers to pray with what appears to be a complete expression of "faith" but is really only presumption.

When God speaks in faith, He speaks always **within the guidelines** of His goals, desires and will. We have to do the same, if we wish to pray with the God-kind of faith. We are not really praying with the God-kind of the faith if we attempt to "trust" Him to do things that are not His goals or desires.

THE PRESUMPTION OF THE ISRAELITES

A good example of presumption is the Israelites' words and actions in Numbers 14:39-45. In these verses, we can see that the Israelites decided to try to enter the Promised Land of Canaan and fight against the heathens there. Previous to this, most Israelites had allowed unbelief and lack of obedience to God's instructions—the Word of the Lord to them—to control them to such a degree that they wouldn't go in to possess the land God had promised them.

After Moses told them what would happen to them because of their unbelief in the Word of the Lord, the same Israelites got involved in thoughts and actions of presumption. They belatedly decided (see Numbers 14:40) that they would go into the Promised Land on the basis of God's Promise made years earlier.

This supposed acting on the Promise of God was not done in faith and obedience. In Numbers 14:21-35, God had told the same people that because of their unbelief and disobedience to His will, it was no longer His will for them to go into and conquer Canaan. As revealed in Numbers 14:40, these men said that they were going to act on God's Promise. This was presumption because they were not now acting according to God's will. Verse 44 says:

> "But they PRESUMED to go up."
> (Revised Standard Version)

God didn't support them with His power when they stepped out in so-called "faith". They were beaten by the Canaanites as a result.

DAVID AVOIDED PRESUMPTION

King David knew how to avoid praying with presumption. In 1 Chronicles 17:25, he revealed a secret of godly prayers of faith. This verse is part of David's prayer to God which can be read in 1 Chronicles 17:16-27. In verse 25, he says:

> "For You, O my God, HAVE TOLD Your servant that You will build him a house (a blessed posterity); THEREFORE Your servant has found COURAGE and CONFIDENCE TO PRAY before You."
> (Amplified Version)

This verse reveals that David had confidence and faith that God would perform a miracle in relation to his descendants. David had this confidence **because God had revealed to him** that it was God's will for this miracle to occur. David had found out God's will from Nathan the prophet (see 1 Chronicles 17:3-15). 1 Chronicles 17:3 says:

> "And that same night the WORD OF GOD came to Nathan..." (Amplified Version)

In New Testament times, we don't have to go to the prophets to find God's will. God the Holy Spirit within each Christian and His Words in the Bible, are our means of finding out what God the Father wants us to ask Him to do for us. We don't understand His character if we doubt that He wants to show us His will. He is **more willing to guide us** of His will than we are to be guided. John 14:26 says of the Holy Spirit:

> "...He will teach you all things. And He will cause

64

*you to recall—will remind you of, bring to your remem-
brance—everything I have told you."*
(Amplified Version)

The Holy Spirit wants to guide us **every hour** of **every
day**. (Refer to Chapter 15, "Day to Day Practice of Seeking
God's Will", and Chapter 10, "The God-Given Mind...
What is it For?" of my book, "HOW TO RECOGNIZE
GOD'S VOICE" for details on what this means.)

If a person says that he knows God's will for us, we
should not accept what he says if it disagrees with the teachings of the Scriptures or God the Holy Spirit hasn't already
revealed to us the same message. God wants to lead us Himself by His Scriptures and by His Holy Spirit within us. On
the rare occasions that He does give a message to someone
else for us, it will be merely a **confirmation** of what He is
already showing us. Many people over the centuries have
been tricked by false prophets and false revelations. We
must be careful!

JOHN 15:7

John 15:7 is a verse which reveals the secret of getting
our requests to God answered:

*"If you live in Me—abide vitally united to Me—and
MY WORDS remain in you and continue to live in
your hearts, ask whatever you will and it SHALL be
done for you."*   *(Amplified Version)*

This Scripture reveals that if we are born again of the
Holy Spirit, and He has revealed to us a specific Word of
the Lord, we can be **100% sure** that He will answer our
request if it is based on this personal Word of the Lord.
The key to answered prayer is **requesting things in response
to Words of the Lord** spoken to us by the ways that God the
Holy Spirit reveals His will to us. The Lord can't refuse to
honour His own Word. As God says:

*"So shall My WORD be that goes forth out of My
mouth; it shall not return to Me void—without produc-
ing any effect, useless."*
(Isaiah 55:11, Amplified Version)

We need to understand that the phrases "the Word of
the Lord" and "the Word of God" have a number of meanings. The Word of God is the **whole Bible.** It is also a **spe-**

cific small revelation of God's will to a **specific person.** For example, when it says in the Old Testament that the Word of the Lord came to a particular person (see Genesis 15:1, 15:4, 1 Kings 6:11), this doesn't mean that God sent him a Bible. It means that God the Holy Spirit spoke to the person's mind what His will was. However, a true, individual Word of the Lord will never contradict the teachings of the Bible as a whole. (Refer to my book, "HOW TO RECOGNIZE GOD'S VOICE", for more details of this.)

A COMMON MISTAKE

There are many Christians who say that what they do in their lives, evangelism, witnessing and praying is based on how the Bible defines faith. But some of these Christians **act** and **pray** in **presumption** and not in real Biblical faith because their prayers and actions are not the result of spending time waiting on God in prayer and constant Bible study, day by day desiring to know God's will. Their prayers and actions are based mostly on their own fleshly goals and desires.

Our God desires every Christian to act and pray only according to His will. Romans 8:26 shows this:

> *"So too the (Holy) Spirit comes to our aid and bears us up in our weakness; for we do not know **what** prayer to offer nor **how** to offer it worthily as we ought..."*
> *(Amplified Version)*

Without the help and guidance of His Holy Spirit, many (if not all) our requests to God will not be based on His will, because **we don't know what we should pray for** nor **how we should pray.** I repeat: we should find out from God **what** He wants us to pray and **how** He wants us to pray. Then we should **obey** Him by praying what He wants and how He wants us to pray.

PRESUMPTION RESULTS IN UNANSWERED REQUESTS

Christians who pray in presumption with what they call "faith", but which is not real Biblical faith, will sometimes say God hasn't answered their requests. I've seen this lead to backsliding a number of times.

I've heard people say, "But I prayed that God would allow me to marry so and so. I prayed in faith, trusting that God would give me anything I asked in Jesus' Name. But God failed me. He didn't answer. Christianity mustn't be real." These people are prayer failures, because they don't **seek constantly to pray according to God's will.**

I've heard others say, "I asked God to make me very rich. I asked in faith, but God didn't answer." Either their prayer wasn't according to God's will, or the person didn't know how to exercise God-inspired faith even though the desire to be a very rich person was God's will. God will only answer prayers based on His will in 99% of cases.

"GOD, MAKE THEM DO YOUR WILL!"

A Christian parent may have grown-up children facing problems in their marriages. There may be violence and much bitterness caused by the spouse's selfishness—or by both parties. The children may have desires about the spending of money, their sexual relationship, where to live, what size house they wish to purchase, and many other things—and fight with their spouse about their differences. Both may not have committed their desires to God's control and asked what He wants.

It is obviously not God's perfect will that this young married couple act in this way towards one another. But because God has given the young couple each free will, He has to allow them to reap the results of their own selfishness.

After being told of the violence and bitterness, the Christian parent may then cry out to God asking Him to solve the problem. The parent may ask God to stop the violence and bitterness within a few days—forcing them to stop sinning.

I have seen many people pray like this and when God does not seem to answer such a request they:

- get bitter or angry with God, or
- feel that God does not love them enough to answer their requests, or
- feel that God has favourites—as though He loves others more than them, or
- think that they have not been good enough or obedient enough to supposedly "earn" an answer from God, or
- condemn themselves thinking they have not got enough faith.

Such prayers are presumption. This is because **nowhere**

67

in the Scriptures does God **promise specifically** that He will solve the problems in our families by forcing them to do His will, when our family members do not wish to obey the teachings of His Scriptures and the guidance of His Holy Spirit. Also, **nowhere in the Scriptures** does God promise specifically that He will answer a request in the number of hours or days or years we request.

Christian parents have Biblical authority to trust God to speak to their son or daughter and spouse—convicting them of their sins (see John 16:7) —and to speak to them about their need to give their lives to His control and about similar things (see John 16:12-15, Revelation 3:1-6). The parents have Biblical authority to engage in spiritual warfare with the demons who are attacking the minds of their children and spouses (see Ephesians 6:10-18, Luke 10:19). But unless the Holy Spirit guides the parent to trust the Father to do something more specific, expecting God to do something more specific than this is presumption.

This is why we must be careful how we interpret Christian testimony books, which tell of how God worked miraculously in the lives of various people. Some of these books are exceptionally helpful. However, some of them give the false impression that because God helped in a specific way in a particular situation, that He will always work in the same way. This creates a false expectation in the minds of the books' readers.

Such books tend to interpret the Scriptures in terms of the miraculous **experiences** of their authors. This is wrong. We need to **judge our experiences** by the Scriptures.

DISCOURAGEMENT AND DISAPPOINTMENT

I have been tremendously burdened in recent years seeing the enormous and unnecessary disappointment and discouragement that has resulted in many Christians' lives I've known, through them following the teachings of some of these well-known American preachers. Some are godly men to varying degrees, who unknowingly or knowingly encourage presumption. After hearing or reading these teachings, some Christians have been discouraged exceptionally when God has not done what they asked Him to do in so-called "faith". The books or sermons these Christians read or heard mention only wonderful testimonies of God doing what others asked, but failed to quote testimonies which show that in 99% of cases, God grants only requests that are specifically His will.

This burden is one of the main reasons the Holy Spirit led me to write this book.

CONCLUDING COMMENTS

Increasingly, there is coming a heavy responsibility on Pentecostal and Charismatic churches:

- to teach about the enormous danger of presumption and similar teachings which are associated with trying to have God build up our own flesh-inspired little kingdoms, and
- to teach its Biblical alternative.

Churches who have experienced great revival and church growth may not continue to do so, unless they take steps to prevent many of their members from falling into presumption and similar fleshly errors that at present, are **masquerading** as forms of "devotion to God."

A church that is experiencing church growth and some level of revival at present may think, "We will never decline." But that is probably what the Methodists said in the 1800's when they were experiencing great revival and growth. Look at the majority of Methodist churches today. They are only a shadow of what they once were.

Throughout history, God has by-passed many local churches and almost entire Christian denominations who have begun to resist His Holy Spirit by beginning to build in many different ways their own "little religious kingdoms" instead of His Kingdom alone.

FOOTNOTES:
1. Ken Chant, THRONE RIGHTS, Vision College Ltd, Australia, 1980, P.79.
2. In English, the word "dream" also refers to the natural occurrence which happens in the mind of every sleeping human.

9
Asking Outside Of God's Will

In 99% of cases, God the Father will not answer presumption prayer requests. But even when He does, things will not work as well for ourselves or those for whom we pray, as if we had prayed according to His revealed perfect will.

This is seen in the following two examples. They are the clearest examples I'm aware of recorded in the Scriptures, of God answering prayers of presumption. There could be others. Study these and see the sad results of these requests being answered.

A REQUEST FOR A KING

The first example in the Scriptures of God answering a request that was against His will, is seen in 1 Samuel 8:1-22. Here, we see that the Israelites in the time of the prophet Samuel, requested Samuel, God's representative, to appoint for them a king. Samuel prayed to the Lord about this. 1 Samuel 8:6-9 says:

"Samuel was displeased with their request for a king; so he prayed to the Lord, and the Lord said, 'Listen to everything the people say to you. You are not the one they have rejected; I am the one they have rejected as their king. Ever since I brought them out of Egypt, they have turned away from Me and worshipped other gods; and now they are doing to you what they have always done to Me. So then, listen to them, but give them strict warnings and explain how their kings will treat them'." *(Good News Version)*

God answered their request, but as shown by 1 Samuel

8:10-18, He revealed to Samuel the terrible sufferings that the kings they had asked for would inflict upon them in the years ahead. A list of these sufferings is recorded in 1 Samuel 8:11-18. God, in his incredible knowledge, could foresee all the evils that these kings would do to the nation of Israel. But because the Israelites insisted that their request was right, in this instance, He gave them what they asked. God did this **even though He clearly said it was not His will** (see 1 Samuel 12:17-20).

This example clearly shows how wrong it is to ask for anything that we want, when selfishly what we ask is not His perfect will. God can foresee the terrible problems that will result for us, if He gives us some of the things we selfishly desire. We are often like a child who asks his parent if he can play on a road which has many cars speeding on it.

BALAAM

In order to understand the following, please read beforehand Numbers Chapters 22 to 24, 2 Peter 2:15-16, Jude 11, Joshua 13:22, Numbers 31:15-16 and Revelation 2:14. This is necessary, especially if you are not familiar with the life of Balaam.

Balaam was a prophet according to the Apostle Peter (see 2 Peter 2:15-16). As revealed by Numbers 24:1 and Joshua 13:22, however, Balaam practiced also divination, fortune-telling and occult. In ancient times, those who practiced such evil things sometimes obtained great riches as payment from those who consulted them. This selfish craving after riches resulted in Balaam wanting God to change His will about a particular matter. This matter involved the nations of Moab, Midian and Israel.

When the nation of Moab, their king called Balak and their allies— the Midianites—saw that the nation of Israel had camped on the plains of Moab, they were terrified. They had heard how the Israelites had annihilated the armies of two other pagan nations who had attacked the Israelites.

As a result, King Balak sent some of his men to see Balaam. As recorded in Numbers 22:5-6, Balak had these messengers ask Balaam to put a curse on the nation of Israel. To encourage Balaam to do this, King Balak sent a payment to be given to him (see Numbers 22:7).

When the Moabite and Midianite leaders sent by King Balak arrived at Balaam's place, they gave him King Balak's message. In answer, Balaam told them he would see whatever the Lord would reveal to him about the matter. He had them stay at his place overnight. Balaam prayed to the Lord about the matter. In reply, the Lord said:

> *"Do not go with these men, and do not put a curse on the people of Israel, because they have my blessing."*
> *(Numbers 22:12—Good News Version)*

At this point, Balaam obeyed God. He told King Balak's messengers to go back home. He did not let the temptation of great financial reward get a hold of him.

So King Balak devised another evil scheme. He sent a larger number of important leaders of the Moabites and Midianites to Balaam. As Numbers 22:16-17 records:

> *"They went to Balaam and gave him this message from Balak: 'Please don't let anything prevent you from coming to me! I will reward you richly and do anything you say. Please come and curse these people for me.'"*
> *(Good News Version)*

Balaam Wanted God To Change His Mind

At first glance, the prophet Balaam's answer to them **appears** to be a very godly answer. Numbers 22:18-19 records this:

> *"And Balaam answered the servants of Balak, If Balak would give me his house full of silver and gold, I cannot go beyond the word of the Lord my God, to do less or more. Now therefore, I pray you, tarry here again tonight that I may know what more the Lord will say to me."* *(Amplified Version)*

The first part of Balaam's answer seems to indicate that he wanted to obey God in even the smallest thing. But we must remember that God had previously clearly revealed that His will was for Balaam not to go with them and not to curse the people of Israel. Therefore, despite all of his godly talk, Balaam was desiring God to change His mind about this matter. This is why Balaam's words about wanting to see if the Lord had something else to say were godly only on the surface. Balaam had a selfish desire of wanting God to change His will, so that he could become very financially

73

prosperous through King Balak's payments. 2 Peter 2:15-16 reveals this:

> *"They have left the straight path and have lost their way; they have followed the path taken by Balaam son of Beor, who LOVED THE MONEY he would get for doing wrong and was rebuked for his sin. His donkey spoke with a human voice and stopped the prophet's insane action."*   *(Good News Version)*

Jude 11 confirms this:

> *"How terrible for them! They have followed the way that Cain took. For the sake of money they have given themselves over to the error that Balaam committed...."*   *(Good News Version)*

Numbers 22:19 reveals that Balaam wanted to wait on God in prayer about this same matter again—hoping that He would change His mind. Since Balaam had such a strong desire to go with the Moabite and Midianite princes to where King Balak was, Numbers 22:20 reveals that God told him to go with them.

God Reveals His Perfect Will A Second Time

Even though the Lord had told Balaam that he had the Lord's permission to go with King Balak's princes, this was not the Lord's perfect will. Numbers 22:22 reveals this:

> *"God was angry that Balaam was going, and as Balaam was riding along on his donkey, accompanied by his two servants, the angel of the Lord stood in the road to bar his way."*   *(Good News Version)*

Balaam was so keen to get to King Balak that he became furious with his donkey. He began to beat his donkey with a stick. How similar this is to many of us? We have some selfish desire that is not God's perfect will. We ask the Lord to grant us the fulfillment of our desire. We become angry with anyone or anything that gets in the road of the fulfillment of our desire. James 4:1-3 speaks also of this.

Numbers 22:31-32 reveals that a second time, the Lord revealed that it was not His will for Balaam to go to Balak:

> *"Then the Lord opened Balaam's eyes, and he saw the Angel of the Lord standing in the way with His sword drawn in His hand; and he bowed his head,*

*and fell on his face. And the Angel of the Lord said
to him, Why have you struck your donkey these three
times? See, I came out to STAND AGAINST AND
RESIST YOU, for your behaviour is WILLFULLY
OBSTINATE and CONTRARY before me."*
(Amplified Version)

Then we see recorded in Numbers 22:34 that Balaam
admitted that he had sinned in wanting to go to King Balak.
Numbers 22:34 says:

*"Balaam said to the Angel of the Lord, I have sinned;
for I did not know You stood in the way against me.
But now, if my going displeases You, I will return."*
(Amplified Version)

Here Balaam admits that he was sinning in going to King
Balak. But note **he does not repent totally** in his actions.
He does not say that he is going to return immediately
home. Instead, he reveals that if God instructs His Angel
to insist that he returns home, he will. But if God has His
angel tell Balaam to continue to go to Balak, he will gladly
do so. The Lord could see by this that Balaam still wanted
to go to Balak. So the Lord had His Angel tell Balaam to
go to King Balak (see Numbers 22:35).

Once Balaam reached King Balak, we see that for a
period of time, Balaam allowed himself to be God's vessel
in speaking the Word of the Lord. His words recorded in
Numbers 22:38 indicate this.

Then we see in Numbers Chapters 23 and 24 that Balaam
sought the Lord's will about what to prophesy about the
nation of Israel. Balaam was willing to say whatever the
Lord told him about Israel. Balaam was willing even to tell
King Balak that the Lord said that one day, the Israelites
would conquer the people of Moab (see Numbers 24:16-17).

Doing an Enormous Evil For Riches

But do not think that the story ends here. As recorded
in the next chapter in the Book of Numbers, the women from
King Balak's Moab and from the Midianite tribes invited the
men of Israel to attend their pagan sacrificial feasts. These
women tempted them to come by offering to have sexual
intercourse with them (see Numbers 25:1-3). This caused
some of the Israelite men to turn away from God. Other
related problems occurred also.

Who encouraged the Moabites and the Midianites to send many of their women to trap some of the Israelite men in this way? The answer is given in Numbers 31:15-16, where it records Moses said about the Midianite women that the Israelite army had captured:

> *".... Why have you kept all the women alive? Remember that it was the women who followed Balaam's instructions and at Peor led the people to be unfaithful to the Lord. That was what brought the epidemic on the Lord's people."*   (Good News Version)

Revelation 2:14 confirms this:

> *"But there are a few things I have against you: there are some among you who follow the teaching of Balaam, WHO TAUGHT BALAK HOW TO LEAD THE PEOPLE OF ISRAEL INTO SIN by persuading them to eat food that had been offered to idols and to practice sexual immorality."*   (Good News Version)

This verse reveals that the prophet Balaam was the one who taught King Balak how to lead the people of Israel into sin. So either during the period Balaam was uttering the wonderful prophecies spoken of in Numbers Chapters 23 and 24 and was speaking other godly words (see Numbers 23:12, 26; 24:13) or after then, Balaam must have done this enormously wicked thing.

You may ask why Balaam did this. The answer is his selfish over-emphasis on riches and money.

The example of Balaam is a **clear warning** to us all of the danger of allowing some selfish desire to lead us to ask the Lord to do something for us contrary to His will.

THE SEEDS OF POSSIBLE BACKSLIDING

If we try to use God to fulfil our selfish desires, we will very often backslide. This is because self-reliance, self-centredness and lack of trust that God knows what is best for us—all underlying our selfish desire— will act like an **infected sore.** If it is not gotten rid of, by being given over to God's control, it and its roots of self-reliance, lack of trust and so on may come to control us so much that we backslide.

I have seen such backsliding take two forms. I have seen people stop going to church altogether or go only on rare occasions. Others have continued to go regularly to church but have backslidden—lost a lot of their devotion and love for God—in their thoughts and hearts.

God is pleased to allow Christians to make money, have a successful business, play sport, buy material possessions, seek good careers, be educated, buy nice clothes, have a nice physical appearance and so on. This is as long as they desire to love and value Him above these things. But I've seen quite a number of Christians backslide because they **tried to use God**—asking and exercising what they thought was "Biblical faith" for Him to satisfy their selfish desires. These selfish desires were not based on glorifying God or on extending His Kingdom in their lives or in the lives of others.

Charles Finney's Comments

When referring to teaching and discipling new converts, the great American evangelist Charles Finney of the 1800's said, "If young converts are not well instructed, they will **inevitably backslide.**"[1] In another place, he said, "And where religious character grows feeble, rely upon it, in nine cases out of ten it is owing to their being neglected, or falsely instructed, when they were young converts."[2]

When talking about what dedication to God is, Finney said, "Young converts should be taught that they have renounced the ownership of all their **possessions,** and of **themselves.**......They should not be left to think that anything is their own; their **time, property, influence, faculties, body** or **soul.** 'Ye are not your own' (1 Corinthians 6:19), they belong to God; and when they submitted to God they made a free surrender of **all** to Him... They have no right to spend one hour as if their time were their own; no right to **go anywhere** or **do anything** for themselves, but should hold all at the disposal of God, and employ all for the glory of God."

"If God calls on them to employ anything they have, their money, or their time, or to give their children or to dedicate themselves in advancing His Kingdom; and they refuse, because they want to use them in their own way or prefer to do something else, it is vastly more blameable than for a clerk or an agent to go and embezzle the money that is entrusted him by his employer."[3]

"They should be made to understand that **nothing which is selfish** is (true Christian[4]) religion...A man may just as much commit sin in praying, or reading the Bible, or going

77

to a religious service, if his **motive** is selfish."[5]

Finney is not saying here that it is sinful to eat food, enjoy sleep, have a house, own material possessions, get married, have a sexual relationship with a wife or husband and enjoy talking to people. We are not told to live by ourselves in a cave or sleep on sharp nails. Finney is saying do we eat, sleep and so on for selfish reasons or because God wants us to do these things? It depends on our **motive**. As 1 Corinthians 10:31 says:

> *"So then, whether you eat or drink, or whatever you may do, do all for the honor and glory of God."*
> *(Amplified Version)*

It is a sad fact also that many of the American television ministries that have spoken so much about faith, prayer and miracles are the ones who have laid some **seeds of backsliding** in thousands of Pentecostal and Charismatic Christians in many nations. Many of these preachers have desired rightly to see thousands be converted and never backslide, the churches grow and people to have miraculous answers to prayer. But by not emphasizing enough the importance of having **holy motives** for wanting God to do miraculous things for us, these preachers have given the impression that God does not mind us keeping our selfish desires and self-reliant ways. They have not taught that God requires us to have **a holy faith** (see Jude 20).

A Holy Faith

The Biblical words "faith" and "holiness" go together. A "holy faith" is defined as a faith that is **separated** from the desires of Satan and the non-Christian world's ways of using God's natural and spiritual creation. A "holy faith" is a faith that is **dedicated** to **God's use** and **purposes.** (Refer to my book "KEYS TO KNOWING GOD BETTER" for a deeper understanding of what is holiness, dedication to God and separation from what the Bible calls "the world".)

Exercising faith for miracles is not some mystical realm divorced from holy motives.

Looking for Books and Preachers That Support Our Selfishness

Many of us are like the people of Israel in Samuel's time who asked for a king. The Lord has not said that what we want is His best for us, but we still want it anyway. We look for books and preachers who tell us that God will give us whatever we desire, if we follow a certain so-called "Biblical" formula that the book or preacher is famous for in Christian circles. Then we use this formula, trying to force God to give us what we want. Then the Lord decides to let us have the fruit of our sinful desire. He does this with the hope that we will come to realize how foolish it is for us to put our own selfish desires above His desires for our lives. God continues to try to lead us to repent of this selfish desire.

Some people come to realize that their selfish desire was not as wonderful as they thought. As a result, they repent, give it to God's control and begin to desire only what He wants for them. However, sadly, others go deeper and deeper into self-reliance, self-centredness and lack of love for God.

CONCLUDING REMARKS

On rare occasions, if you keep asking God for something that is not His will, with great sadness in His heart, He may give you what selfishly you ask. But remember, **don't blame Him** when you see develop the unnecessary, great problems and troubles that result from your foolish request.

Asking God for something that is not His perfect will, always results in trouble. This trouble may not develop at first. Things may work well for a while. However, sooner or later, some form of unnecessary trouble will result.

FOOTNOTES:
1. Charles Finney, "REVIVAL LECTURES", Fleming H. Revell Company, Old Tappan, New Jersey, United States, P. 485.
2. Ibid, P.484.
3. Ibid, P.454-455.
4. This is my inclusion because the word "religion" has many meanings.
5. Finney, op.cit.,P.469.

10
God's Will Is Best

Some of us are like Lazarus' sisters. We start off asking God for something which is not His will. But then God reveals that His will for us is **even better** than what we originally asked for.

Lazarus' sisters originally asked the Lord Jesus to heal their brother. The fact that they sent a message to the Lord saying that Lazarus was sick (see John 11:3) and that they had previously seen and heard of the Lord healing all other sick people who asked Him to heal them, indicates that the sisters' message to Him implied that they were wanting Him to heal Lazarus. This is confirmed by the fact that in John 11:21-22, Martha said the following words:

> *"Martha said to Jesus, 'If you had been here, Lord, my brother WOULD NOT HAVE DIED! But I know that even now God will give you whatever you ask for'."*
> *(Good News Version)*

Mary, Lazarus' other sister, had the same attitude (see John 11:32).

When the sisters' request came to Him, Jesus **did not give them what they asked.** He did not give them what they asked because He knew that the Father's will for Lazarus and them was **far better** than what they were asking. John 11:4 shows this:

> *"When Jesus heard it, he said, 'The final result of this sickness will not be the death of Lazarus; this has happened in order to bring glory to God, and it will be the means by which the Son of God will receive glory'."*
> *(Good News Version)*

The Father wanted not just to heal Lazarus, but to raise

Him from the dead as well. The Lord Jesus did not immediately command the sickness to leave Lazarus or go to Lazarus' bedside straight away. In **obedience to the Father,** He waited two more days.

The raising of Lazarus from the dead achieved far more than if Jesus had answered the sisters' original request for healing alone. This miracle resulted in many people believing in Jesus (see John 11:45) and brought great glory to the Father (see John 11:4).

The problem for many of us is that we think that if we seek to pray only according to God's will, He will often want us to have things that are not best for us. We may think that if we ask God for bread when we have no food left, He will give us a stone and let us starve to death. Jesus in Matthew 7:9-11 says that human fathers, who are influenced by much selfishness and sin, would not give to their children something which is worse for them than what they originally asked for. From this, Jesus then argues **how much more** does God the Father wish to give, **not things that are worse** for us than what we ask, but **better**:

> *"Would any of you who are fathers give your son a stone when he asks for bread? Or would you give him a snake when he asks for a fish? As bad as you are, you know how to give good things to your children. HOW MUCH MORE, then, will your Father in heaven give GOOD THINGS to those who ask Him?"*
> *(Good News Version)*

Many don't believe the Bible as much as theological books and books about the lives of so-called "holy" men and "Saints". From these books, they sometimes form false notions about God's will and His character, ideas they will not find in His Scriptures. They need to reject teachings and practices spoken of in these books which are contrary to the teachings of the Scriptures. As a result of accepting these false ideas, they do not realize that as verses such as Ephesians 3:20, Matthew 23:37 and 2 Samuel 12:7-8 hint, God wants to do FAR MORE and BETTER things for us than what we would even ask for ourselves.

We must learn to recognize the guidance of the Holy Spirit; otherwise we will have little awareness when He is trying to lead us to trust the Father to provide something which is better for us than what we originally asked for.

KING SOLOMON

1 Kings 3:5-14 reveals another Scriptural example of God giving to someone not just specifically what they asked. King Solomon asked just for the wisdom needed to rule the nation of Israel with justice and to know the difference between good and evil. But God gave Solomon **more than he asked.** Verses 12 and 13 reveal this:

"I will do what you have asked. I will give you more wisdom and understanding than anyone has ever had before or will ever have again. I will ALSO GIVE YOU WHAT YOU HAVE NOT ASKED FOR: all your life you will have wealth and honor, more than that of any other king." (Good News Version)

God's will for Solomon **was better** than what Solomon asked for himself.

The examples of Lazarus and Solomon disprove another false teaching that I've heard in recent years—the idea that God will give us no more or no less than what specifically we ask of Him.

But do not take this to mean that I'm suggesting God's will will always be something different from what we ask of Him. Sometimes, when we ask God for some specific thing, He will speak to us by His Spirit confirming that this is His will. At other times, He may reveal to us that what we ask is not His will and He wishes to do something for us far better than we ask.

11
Difference Between Natural And Biblical Faith

One of the main reasons why a number of Christians have been caught in the trap of praying in presumption when they thought that they were praying in Biblical faith, is that they have not known there is a **big** difference between natural faith and Holy Spirit-inspired Biblical faith.

NATURAL FAITH

Natural faith is expressed when we trust that the chair that we are sitting on will not collapse. We base this natural faith on our **experiences** over many years of seeing well-made chairs not collapse. If we have had a bad experience once when a chair that we were sitting on collapsed, we might doubt that other chairs will hold us up.

Other examples of natural faith are when we believe that the aeroplane that we are flying in will get us from one city to another destination, the roof of the house that we are living in will not collapse on top of us, the television set will have pictures on it when we switch it on and the food that we have bought has not got poison in it.

Our natural faith in these examples is based on a combination of the **experiences** of our **eyes, ears** and **other physical senses,** the **reasoning** of our **own mind** and what other people have taught us from their **physical sense experiences** and **their reasonings.** Such faith is not evil, but it is purely a natural thing. It is not faith as defined in the Bible because it is not based upon a revelation of God's will as found in His Bible or by the guidance of His Holy Spirit.

Natural faith is **a gift of God,** but it is **limited** in that it is based upon the limited reasonings of our and other people's minds and physical sense experiences. Natural faith is of **little use** in the realm of praying for miracles. In fact, it **often tries to oppose** an expression of Biblical faith, when our human reason and common sense (formed on the basis of our experiences in life) tell us that what God reveals He wants us to ask Him for is impossible.

Refer to Chapters 10 and 12 of my book, "HOW TO RECOGNIZE GOD'S VOICE", for many details and examples of this.

Many people think that they are praying in God-inspired Biblical faith when they are really not. They are trying to use their natural faith in the realm of praying for miracles. Other people go from one type of faith to the other. They pray with Biblical faith for various miracles and see wonderful results. Then at other times, they try to pray with natural faith and see no miracles resulting. They then wonder what is wrong. They don't know why sometimes God answers their requests and then at other times, refuses to answer. They are often confused as a result.

One (but not the only) reason why many Christians confuse natural faith with Holy Spirit-inspired Biblical faith is the false idea that every human is given a certain amount of Biblical faith when they are born. This teaching suggests that even unbelievers are given a measure of Biblical faith by God. The main Scripture which is used supposedly to prove this false teaching is Romans 12:3:

> *"For by the grace (unmerited favor of God) given to me I warn every one among you not to estimate and think of himself more highly than he ought—not to have an exaggerated opinion of his own importance; but to rate his ability with sober judgement, each according to the degree of faith APPORTIONED BY GOD to him."* (Amplified Version)

The Authorized Version translates the latter part of this verse as, *".... according as God hath dealt to every man the MEASURE OF FAITH."* When we look at the words, *"God hath dealt to every man the MEASURE OF FAITH"* **in context** with the rest of the verse 3 and verses 4-5, we see what these words are really saying.

In the first part of verse 3, we see a hint of those to

whom the Apostle Paul was directing his words. Paul says, *"I warn every one among you."* These words are not referring to the whole human race, unbelievers included. But as verses 4 and 5 of the same chapter show, they are referring to the body of Christ—the born-again sons and daughters of God.

Romans 12:1 proves that verse 3 is only talking about born-again Christians, because the Apostle Paul directs his comments which follow in the rest of this chapter to a particular group. Romans 12:1 begins with:

> *"I appeal to you therefore, BRETHREN, and beg of you...."*　　　　　　　　　*(Amplified Version)*

Paul did not make it a habit to call unbelievers by the words "brethren" or "brothers." (The only exceptions to this are recorded in Acts 13:26, 13:38, 22:1, 23:1, 23:5-6 and 28:17. In these instances, Paul addressed non-Christian religious male Jews with the word "brothers." But his usage of this word in these instances related to Paul's common ancestry with other Jews—his brothers in race. As revealed by Paul's words recorded in Romans 2:17-29, 10:1-3, Acts 28:25-29 and other parts of the New Testament, he did not regard non-Christian Jews as being brothers in Christ though.)

Likewise, Paul at the beginning of the Book of Romans explained to whom his comments in the rest of the Book were directed. He said in Romans 1:7:

> *"To (you then) all God's beloved ones in Rome, called to be SAINTS and DESIGNATED FOR A CONSECRATED LIFE..."*　　　　　　*(Amplified Version)*

Paul did not ever include unbelievers in his definition of a saint of God.

Another verse which proves that not all humans have Biblical faith within them—the ability to trust God for salvation, guidance, miracles or anything else—is 2 Thessalonians 3:2:

> *"And that we may be delivered from unreasonable and wicked men: for ALL MEN HAVE NOT FAITH."*
> 　　　　　　　　　　　　　*(Authorized Version)*

Someone might argue that James 2:19 says that demons

believe, but they have not got the Lord Jesus or His faith within them.

But the believing spoken of here is merely believing **mentally** that God exists, there is only one God, He is all-powerful and so on. James 2:19 is not talking about the Lord Jesus' faith. Jesus' faith within a demon would cause it to have a personal relationship to God the Father. But since demons hate God and want no personal love relationship to Him, this reveals they do not have the Lord Jesus' faith within them.

Nowhere in the Scriptures does it say that God has given all people a measure of faith. Only born-again Christians have this gift.

God desires that every human allow Him to give them Jesus' faith. 1 Timothy 2:3-4 and Ephesians 2:8 infer this. This divinely imparted ability to believe—trust and rely—in God the Father is given to us the moment we agree to receive Jesus Christ into ourselves as Our Lord and Saviour. He offers Himself to us and when we respond by accepting Him, we also receive **His faith** within us.

BIBLICAL FAITH

Faith in the Biblical sense of the word is something which the Lord Jesus Christ living within us **inspires in us** and **imparts to us.** This does not mean that the Lord Jesus will do all of our praying to the Father for us. The Scriptures say that Jesus will intercede for us many times with the Father (see 1 John 2:1). But also on many occasions, the Scriptures command us to pray (see Ephesians 6:18, 1 Thessalonians 5:17), and to express faith in God (see Ephesians 6:16, Proverbs 3:5). We must pray willingly to God the Father and exercise faith in Him, while allowing His Scriptures and the Lord Jesus within us to inspire and motivate **what** and **how** we pray.

When we are born-again of the Holy Spirit, we receive Jesus Christ to live within us (see Colossians 1:27, Romans 8:9, 1 John 3:24). When we receive Jesus Christ into our spirit and body, we don't receive a quarter or a half or any other fraction of Jesus. We receive a **whole** Jesus.[1] When we dedicate our lives to Him—asking Him to be Our Lord and Saviour—we receive **all** the faith that He had in God the Father and in the Father's love, power and wisdom. We don't just receive a part of Jesus' faith.

When we are born again, this faith of the Lord Jesus is only in us in **potential** form. It is within us because Christ is within us. But He will only allow this faith to be expressed by us **towards goals and in ways that are the Father's will.**

Proof that this faith of the Lord Jesus in God the Father, which resulted in so many hundreds of amazing miracles in Jesus' life on Earth, comes to be in us when we receive Jesus Christ into our hearts is seen in Galatians 2:20:

"I am crucified with Christ: nevertheless I live; yet not I, but Christ liveth in me; and the life which I now live in the flesh I live by THE FAITH OF THE SON OF GOD, who loved me, and gave Himself for me."
                                        (Authorized Version)

Galatians 2:16 and Mark 11:22 confirm this. In the original Greek, both of these verses use a sentence construction of which there is no English equivalent.[2] In the original Greek, Galatians 2:16 indicates that Jesus Christ is not only the **object** of our faith, but the **source** of it also.[3] In the original Greek, Mark 11:22 expresses that God is not only the **object** of our faith, but also the **source** of it.[4] This is why some versions of the Bible translate these two verses as "faith **in** Jesus Christ" or "faith **in** God", while others translate them as "faith **of** Jesus Christ" or "faith **of** God". (John 5:42 does the same in that it indicates God is both the source of a Christian's love and the object towards which this love is expressed.[5])

But many do not realize that Jesus will not allow His faith within us to be expressed towards any miracle that is not God the Father's will. Jesus' words in John 5:19 show this:

"So Jesus answered them by saying, 'I assure you, most solemnly I tell you, the Son is able to do NOTHING FROM HIMSELF—of His own accord; but He is able to do ONLY WHAT HE SEES THE FATHER DOING. For whatever the Father does is what the Son does IN THE SAME WAY [in His turn]'."
                                        (Amplified Version)

Jesus' words in John 5:30, 8:28, 12:49 and 14:10 reveal similar things.

Some people try to exercise Biblical faith for miracles

from the Father that His Scriptures or the guidance of His Holy Spirit have not specifically revealed are His will. They try to **"work up"** Biblical faith by positive thinking and speaking and by acting in ways that supposedly suggest they are expressing this faith.

But their efforts to exercise Biblical faith are **in vain,** because the Lord Jesus living within them will not allow His faith to inspire and control them in their attempts to get miraculous answers from God the Father. The many previous examples of presumption show this.

JESUS WITHIN US

Some wrongly think that Jesus Christ is only in heaven (see Hebrews 1:3) and in the spiritual world. They are not deeply aware that **the Lord Jesus** and **His faith** lives **inside** every born-of-the-Holy-Spirit-believer, as revealed by such verses as Colossians 1:17:

> *"God's plan is to make known HIS SECRET to his people, this rich and glorious secret which he has for all peoples. And the secret is that CHRIST IS IN YOU, which means that you will share in the glory of God."* (Good News Version)

It is amazing that Jesus Christ can live in us like this. But because He is God, nothing is impossible for Him.

Jesus wants to impart His faith to us by showing us from the Holy Scriptures and the guidance of the Holy Spirit what specifically God the Father wants us to ask Him for. Jesus always wants us to allow His faith to so control our **thoughts**, **words** and **actions** that we will be praying not only what He wants us to pray, but also **how** He wants us to pray. As Hebrews 12:2 says in part:

> *"Looking unto Jesus the AUTHOR and FINISHER OF OUR FAITH...."* (Authorized Version)

This verse is primarily referring to Jesus Christ being the one Who imparts to us the faith that is necessary to have a personal relationship to God the Father and the one Who will help to mature and deepen the outworking of this faith in our lives. But it can refer more specifically to Jesus being **the Giver** of **the faith** and the **knowledge of God's will** needed to be able to pray for miracles the way the Father would want us to.

WORSHIP GOD NOT FAITH

Some Christian authors wrongly teach continually the Biblical concept "Build up your faith" in a way that would infer that we can exercise faith for things that are not specifically God the Father's will. They talk about "my" personal faith as though it is a thing **ruled totally by themselves** and to which the Father must bend whenever He makes a decision. The Bible does talk of **your** personal faith (see James 1:3, 1 Peter 1:7), and **our** personal faith (see 1 John 5:4), but it emphasises faith as being faith in the **Person** of God, **not faith in faith itself**. Some make faith into such a **human effort programme** that they are **worshipping faith,** instead of worshipping God.

CO-OPERATING WITH JESUS WITHIN

We have to co-operate with the Lord Jesus living within us by being willing to allow **His faith** to **inspire** and **rule** our prayer requests for miracles. He will not force us to exercise His faith. After the Lord Jesus has motivated us to use His faith to obtain a particular miracle from the Father, we must then choose to express His faith by believing and speaking that the Father will definitely perform this miracle. If we don't do this, this is sinful doubt.

CURSING THE FIG TREE

Some people argue, "You can't say that when Jesus cursed the fig tree and it miraculously withered up and died (see Mark 11:13-21) that He was guided by God the Father to do this." This argument is seen to be wrong when we consider verses such as John 14:10 where Jesus said:

"Do you not believe that I am in the Father and that the Father is in Me? What I am telling you I do not say on My own authority and of My own accord, but THE FATHER Who lives continually in ME DOES THE WORKS —HIS MIRACLES, HIS OWN DEEDS OF POWER."　　　*(Amplified Version)*

If it was true that God would wither every fig tree or other tree that we cursed and positively confessed and "believed" would wither, even if it was not His will, this would mean that any Christian could go around a nation causing all of its trees to wither, resulting in famine and possibly starvation for thousands of other Christians. God **is not so foolish** as to allow His power to be left available for such irresponsible use.

We are the Lord Jesus' body (see 1 Corinthians 12:12-27). He wants to express Himself through us as His body with the same sorts of miracles, love and wisdom as He expressed when He was here on Earth. This is a great thing that many fail to understand.

THE HOLY SPIRIT

We can speak of the work of the Holy Spirit within us in a similar way to that of Jesus Christ within us. The Holy Spirit knows **everything** about the will of God the Father. 1 Corinthians 2:11 says in part:

> *"...Just so no one discerns (comes to know and comprehend) the thoughts of God except the Spirit of God."*
> *(Amplified Version)*

John 16:13 says that the Holy Spirit will guide us into a knowledge of what God the Father's will is about many things:

> *"But when He, the Spirit of Truth (the truth-giving Spirit) comes, He WILL GUIDE YOU INTO ALL THE TRUTH—the whole, full truth. For He will not speak His own message—on His own authority—but He will tell whatever He hears [from the Father, He will give the message that has been given to Him] and He will announce and declare to you the things that are to come—that will happen in the future."*
> *(Amplified Version)*

Romans 8:26 says that the Holy Spirit will show us what and/or how to pray. Romans 8:27 says that the Holy Spirit will only pray and intercede for Christians **according to God the Father's will:**

> *"So too the (Holy) Spirit comes to our aid and bears us up in our weakness; for we DO NOT KNOW WHAT PRAYER TO OFFER nor HOW to offer it worthily as we ought, but the Spirit Himself goes to meet our supplication and pleads in our behalf with unspeakable yearnings and groanings too deep for utterance. And He Who searches the hearts of men knows what is in the mind of the (Holy) Spirit—what His*

intent is—because the Spirit intercedes and pleads [before God] on behalf of the saints ACCORDING TO and IN HARMONY WITH GOD'S WILL."

(Amplified Version)

These verses together show that the Holy Spirit wishes to lead us how to pray according to God the Father's will. He will not lead us to request things that are not the Father's will. Nor will He inspire or impart the Lord Jesus' faith to us **unless what we are requesting is the Father's will.**

BEFORE THE LORD'S DEATH AND RESURRECTION

In the years before the Lord Jesus died and was resurrected, no one had Him living within them (see Colossians 1:25-27). Neither did any one have the Holy Spirit living within them in the same sense that true Christians would have after Jesus died and was resurrected (see John 7:39, Acts 2:14-18).

But prior to Jesus Christ's death and resurrection, the Holy Spirit was still trying to influence and inspire His faith towards God the Father in people. Acts 7:51, Genesis 6:3 and Isaiah 63:10 indicate this. Biblical faith for a miracle from the Father is something which the Holy Spirit would have had to inspire and give to them, before they could have been sure that the Father would answer their request. Therefore, even in the miracles recorded in the Old Testament and those recorded in the Gospels, the Holy Spirit inspired the faith of those who trusted God to perform these miracles.

FOOTNOTES:

1. Your limited natural human mind may find this hard to understand. This is just as the human mind finds it hard to understand how God could listen to millions of people praying to Him at the same time.

2. Ken Chant, "FAITH DYNAMICS", Vision College Ltd, Australia, 1980, P.14.

3. Ibid.

4. Ibid.

5. Ibid.

12
Rare Instances In Scripture

GOD ANSWERING CONTRARY TO HIS ORIGINALLY STATED WILL

The Bible reveals there are only two types of situations in which God may answer a prayer request that is contrary to what originally He stated was His will[1]:

- On a limited number of occasions, God has been willing to change His will about a matter when a person has asked Him to follow an alternative course of action that will glorify Him and build up His kingdom here on earth in some way.

  Glorifying Him is **honouring** and **valuing Him above everyone** and **everything else** and encouraging others to do this in their thoughts, words and actions also (see 1 Corinthians 10:31). The Kingdom of God relates to God's rule in heaven and the spiritual world (see 2 Timothy 4:18), but it also relates to His ruling over our human spirit, mind and body (see Luke 17:20-21) and over the daily activities of our lives (see Matthew 7:21).

- When a person will not hand over some selfish desire to God's control and foolishly, he asks God to fulfil this desire, the Lord may, in some instances, give him what he asks. Or the Lord may step back and allow him to obtain the fulfillment of this desire himself. Examples of this are given in Chapter 9 "Asking Outside Of God's Will." Instances such as these are **relatively rare.** This is proven by the fact that James 4:3 reveals that

95

mostly if a person asks selfishly, God will not give him what he asks.

PRAYER REQUESTS THAT GLORIFY GOD

Here are some Biblical examples of the Lord being willing to change His stated will because someone asked Him to do something else which glorified Him greatly. In Exodus 33:1-3, it is recorded that the Lord said that He wanted Moses and the people of Israel to leave Mount Sinai and to go to the Promised Land. The Lord said that He would send an angel to guide them and would drive out the pagan nations in the Promised Land. The Lord said also that He would not go with the people of Israel Himself, because of their stubborn hearts and the likelihood of Him judging them severely.

As recorded in Exodus 33:12-17 however, after Moses had discussed this matter with the Lord, the Lord was willing to change His will. Moses told the Lord of some godly reasons why He should continue to have His presence go with them.

It was not that God had not thought of these reasons beforehand. God did not say to Moses, "That's a good suggestion, Moses. Fancy me not thinking of that before." God knows everything about everything.

Nor was it that God is gullible, changeable and easy to manipulate to fit in with our selfish purposes.

Nor was it that God began to think that Moses understood more than Him.

In Numbers 14:11-35, it is recorded that the Lord changed His will in answer to Moses' prayer request again. Numbers 14:20 reveals that in answer to Moses' request, the Lord forgave the people of Israel of their rebellion, constant complaining and lack of trust in Him. God did not allow them to be wiped out by a disease epidemic.

In Exodus 32:1-14, we see that the Lord changed His will again in answer to Moses' prayer request.

There are **relatively few** of these examples recorded in the Scriptures. It is possible to infer from this that God only rarely answers these types of requests.

Difference Between Humbly Asking and Arrogantly Expecting

Note that in the above examples, Moses **humbly asked** the Lord to change His will. Moses **did not arrogantly**

expect God to change His will as though it was some sort of "right". In humility, Moses asked the Lord to change His will, but all the while being willing to accept if He refused to change His will. Moses knew that because he had a love relationship and friendship with the Lord, he could ask the Lord such things. But Moses never lost the attitude that the Lord's answers to his requests would always be the best for everyone.

Note also that in these examples, Moses did not ask because of self-centred, self-glorifying motives. Moses did not treat God as some sort of "spiritual Santa Claus." Moses asked from motives based on glorifying God in the eyes of other people and on expanding God's Kingdom here on Earth.

IT IS UP TO GOD TO DECIDE

We may think that every part of our prayer request is based on glorifying God and building His kingdom here on Earth. But it is up to Him to decide and then reveal by His Holy Spirit which parts of our prayer requests He regards as glorifying Him. Some of us become wrongly impatient with God when He does not do things that we think honour and glorify Him most.

Observe also that on at least two occasions, God told Moses that He would not change His will, even if Moses asked. The first of these examples is recorded in Deuteronomy 3:23-27 (This example is commented on in Chapter 16). The second example is recorded in Exodus 32:30-34. Here Moses said he wanted his name blotted out of the Book—the record God has of those who will be going to heaven—if God would not forgive the people of Israel. God replied that He would not blot anyone's name out of His book for the sort of reason Moses suggested. Compare Exodus 32:32 to Revelation 3:5, Psalm 69:28 and Malachi 3:16-17.

Note also that trusting God for miracles **does not involve nagging Him continually** and then looking day after day at physical circumstances to see if He does what we ask. This is treating prayer **like playing a poker machine**—pulling the prayer handle and seeing if we hit the jackpot. Instead, when we do not know His will, we should first ask Him if the miracle is His will. Then we should wait until the Holy Spirit reveals by His inner guidance whether the miracle is the Father's will.

If the Holy Spirit reveals it is His will, we have then the God-given right to trust Him to perform it. If He reveals that it is not His will, if we have any sense, we will cease asking Him to perform it.

For example, God may tell us that He is going to send an economic depression on a nation to encourage it to repent. We may feel that some other alternative is more glorifying to Him and will extend His Kingdom more. If this is the case, it is far more sensible seeking His Holy Spirit's guidance about whether this alternative is acceptable to Him than in continually asking Him to change His mind and then waiting to see if the economic depression occurs.

If we are relatively sure that our request is glorifying to God, we can share this with Him in prayer. But if by His Spirit, the Lord reveals that our request is not His will, then we must accept that He knows best.

ABRAHAM'S INTERCESSION FOR SODOM AND GOMORRAH

The intercession of Abraham for Sodom and Gomorrah (see Genesis 18:16-33) is an example of God being willing to amend His will in response to the prayer requests of a human intercessor.

But note in this circumstance, it was **God** Who was the One Who **initiated** this discussion between Himself and Abraham over the future of Sodom and Gomorrah. It was **not Abraham** who began this discussion. Genesis 18:17 says:

"And the Lord said to Himself, 'I will not hide from Abraham what I am going to do.'"

(Good News Version)

This infers that if God by His Spirit comes to us on a specific occasion and shares with us something on His heart, He may allow His decision about what He will do to be influenced within **limits** by what we ask of Him. Note also that like Moses, Abraham **humbly asked** the Lord to do as he requested (see Genesis 18:27). Abraham did not arrogantly expect the Lord to do as he asked as some sort of supposed "right."

Also, note that in this instance of Abraham interceding, the Lord allowed His own decision-making to be influenced **only within particular limits.** There was no evil or selfishness in Abraham's request. He asked the Lord to act according

98

to His loving, merciful character in sparing the cities, if the Lord could find in them a number of godly people.

Do you think that if Abraham asked God to give the homosexuals in Sodom and Gomorrah an extra hundred years to be added to each of their lives, for the purpose of them having more chances of participating in perverted acts, that God would have allowed His will to be amended by such a request? What if Abraham asked God to help the men of Sodom to become more violent and full of murder? What if Abraham had asked God to spare some of the homosexual men in Sodom, so that they could become Abraham's sexual partners? Do you think God would have answered such requests? Considering that, as revealed by Chapter 9 "Asking Outside of God's Will," there are only a few examples recorded in the Scriptures of God answering requests based on selfish, evil motives, there would have been only a very small chance of this occurring.

Obviously, God had **limits** on how far He would allow Abraham's requests to influence His final decision. God had the **final say** in the matter, even though He allowed Abraham to discuss with Him **alternatives within these limits.**

God Would Be Unjust

This instance of Abraham interceding with God for Sodom is not an example of God being Abraham's servant and doing whatever Abraham thought was best. In this instance, God was not allowing Abraham to have total say about the fate of thousands of people. God would Himself be **very unjust** if He left the future of the people of Sodom and Gomorrah in the hands of Abraham's human reasoning.

This instance involved the Lord **wanting to share His heart deeply** with His servant, Abraham. God wanted Abraham to communicate deeply with Him.

Also, God wanted to show Abraham how merciful and kind He is, even when confronted with the incredible wickedness of human beings such as those who lived in Sodom and Gomorrah (see Genesis 18:20). By inviting Abraham to discuss with Him the future of the people living in those cities, God was aiming to show how **slow** He is to punish people and how much He always prefers to be loving, merciful and kind to people (see Psalm 103:8, 145:8, Joel 2:13, Jonah 4:2). God was able to use this instance to teach Abraham more things about His character.

As shown here, the intercession of Abraham for Sodom and Gomorrah does not prove that God will give us whatever we ask—no matter how evil or selfish our requests are. Even when He invites us to intercede with Him about a specific matter, He will have **limits** or **boundaries** set on how far He will allow His decision-making to be influenced by what we say.

GOD GAVE DAVID THREE ALTERNATIVES

The Scriptures also reveal that on at least one occasion throughout history, God has given an individual a choice between a number of alternatives. But these are not examples of God changing His will. The only Scriptural example of this I'm aware of is recorded in 1 Chronicles 21:1-30, especially verse 9, where we see God gave King David the choice between three punishments on the nation of Israel.

But note that **God** was the One Who set the choices. Also, it was **He** Who set the limit on the number of choices. God did not give David the right to request any other alternative to these three choices.

GOD ASKS SOLOMON A QUESTION THAT TESTS HIS MOTIVES

In 2 Chronicles 1:7, we see that one night, God came to Solomon and said:

"Ask what I shall give you."   *(Amplified Version)*

In this situation, God's question to Solomon appears to suggest at first that it was God's perfect will to give Solomon anything he asked. But when we see God's response to what Solomon requested, a different picture emerges. In 2 Chronicles 1:11-12, we see that God would not have regarded a selfish request by Solomon for wealth or treasure or fame or death of his enemies or a long life as being a good response. (A desire for wealth, treasure or a long life, however, is not sinful if it is God's will for the person, is not based on selfish motives and the person bases his desire on aiming to extend God's Kingdom among other people.) Solomon asked unselfishly for God to give him God's wisdom and knowledge that were necessary in order to rule God's people properly. We see from verse 11 that God was pleased with his request.

It is not clear from 2 Chronicles 1:11-12 whether if Solomon had asked from selfish motives, God would have answered his request. It is a possibility when we consider what is said in Chapter 9 "Asking Outside of God's Will." Only the Lord knows how He would have responded to such a request. If God had answered such a self-centred request, it would not have been His perfect will.

It is very likely that in this situation, God said to Solomon, *"Ask what I shall give you,"* in order to test his heart's motives. This is hinted at in verse 11, where it is recorded that God responded to Solomon's request by saying, *"Because this was in your heart..."* (Amplified Version). God wanted to see the degree of selfishness or unselfishness that Solomon had at this time. God wanted to know if Solomon's heart desired wealth or treasure or fame or some other thing more than loving, knowing and serving Him.

Note also that 2 Chronicles 1:7-12 reveals that God did not just limit Himself to what Solomon requested. God gave him what he asked for, because his request was based on godly motives. But God gave him more than he requested. God gave him the wealth and fame **that Solomon never requested.** These things reveal that:

- God does not always give us exactly what we ask. Often, **He gives us better**.
- God **looks at our motives** when we ask Him for things.
- He always has the **final say** in any discussion between Him and ourselves about His will for our lives.

OTHER VERSES

There are other verses about these matters which I've heard some people take out of context with the surrounding verses and/or interpret in ways contrary to the teachings of other sections of Scripture. But these cannot all be covered here.

FOOTNOTE:
1. Note that when talking about God changing His will, I'm not inferring that He would ever be willing to change the teachings of His Holy Bible. I'm referring instead to how on some occasions, He has been willing to change His will about matters that He has not revealed His will previously in His Bible.

13
True Intercession

Interceding for others is one facet of requesting the Father to use His miraculous power in the affairs of men. To be an intercessor whose prayer requests are inspired and controlled by the Lord Jesus Christ living within us, we must be willing not to ask God the Father to do something for a family member, a friend or someone else, if Jesus reveals to us that such a request is contrary to the Father's perfect will.

We must be willing to allow the Lord Jesus within us to show us whether such a request is the Father's will. If He tells us not to request such a thing, we must trust Him enough to do what He says.

An example of trust and obedience is seen in the life of Jeremiah. The prophet was told by God not to pray for the people of Judah living at his time. Jeremiah 7:16 says:

"The Lord said, 'Jeremiah, DO NOT PRAY FOR THESE PEOPLE. Do not cry or pray on their behalf; do not plead with Me, for I will not listen to you'."
(Good News Version)

God told Jeremiah instead to believe with certainty that great catastrophies were going to come upon Judah—the land of his birth (see Jeremiah Chapters 14 & 15). Jeremiah had to place his love for God above his loyalty to his parents, family and his country. He had to trust that God knew what was best for the people of Judah. He had to trust that God would know what means were necessary to use to try to get more Judeans to heaven.

In the Bible, it is very rare to find God telling someone not to intercede to Him on behalf of someone else. God is so merciful and kind that He waits and waits and waits for people to turn to Him. But He knows when people have hardened their hearts so much that they will never turn to Him. This is why we must be very sensitive to God's guidance about our intercessions.

We must allow the Lord Jesus living within us to reveal what the Father wants us to ask Him to do for others.

14
Biblical Miracles Without A Word Of The Lord

Sometimes, the Scriptures tell of the historical events of a person trusting God for a miracle, but don't mention that God guided the person to believe in certainty for this miracle. But just because the Scriptures don't record this detail, doesn't mean that this didn't happen. We see a number of examples of this in the Scriptures, for instance this one:

About the year 701 B.C., the Assyrian army under King Sennacherib invaded Judah and surrounded the walled capital Jerusalem. The Assyrians at that time had one of the best armies in the world. However, they were vicious pagans who, by the slow torture of cutting off one part of the body at a time, killed captured opposing soldiers. The Assyrians at this time were far different from those Assyrians who repented in their thousands when Jonah preached to them (see Jonah 3:1-10).

Sennacherib's wicked attitude towards God is seen in 2 Chronicles 32:15. The Assyrian government officials were even more scornful of God (see 2 Chronicles 32:16). They attacked Jerusalem, proudly thinking that the Judean army could not beat them even with God's help. The Assyrians had so easily defeated all other armies, that they thought that the weak little Judean army could never defend Jerusalem properly.

In this desperate situation, 2 Chronicles 32:20-21 says that Hezekiah, king of Judah, and Isaiah the prophet prayed to God. In answer to their trusting prayers, God sent an angel who killed so many Assyrian soldiers that the Assyrian king had to return to his homeland in disgrace:

"Then King Hezekiah and the prophet Isaiah son of Amoz prayed to God and cried out to Him for help. The Lord sent an angel that killed the soldiers and officers of the Assyrian army. So the emperor went back to Assyria disgraced."   *(Good News Version)*

If we just read these verses alone, we may think that they prayed for this specific miracle without first getting guidance from God. It would be easy to make this mistake, because 2 Chronicles 32 nowhere mentions Hezekiah and Isaiah being told by God that it was His will for them to pray with certainty that the Assyrian army would not then capture Jerusalem. If we read these verses only, we could think also mistakenly that Isaiah prayed, "If it be Thy will", or "Lord, I'm hoping You will perform a miracle for Judah."

But if we read the account of the same miracle in 2 Kings 19:20-36, we find that **first** Isaiah waited on God in prayer until he received God's inner guidance that it was His will for Isaiah and Hezekiah to trust Him to prevent the Assyrian army from conquering Jerusalem at this time. 2 Kings 19:32-34 says:

"And this is what THE LORD HAS SAID about the Assyrian emperor: 'He will not enter this city or shoot a single arrow against it. No soldiers with shields will come near the city, and no siege mounds will be built around it. He will go back by the same road he came, without entering this city. I, the Lord, have spoken. I will defend this city and protect it, for the sake of my own honour and because of the promise I made to my servant David'."   *(Good News Version)*

This was what God said to Isaiah and Hezekiah. Romans 10:17 reveals that once these two men had the Word of the Lord on the matter, they had the God-given right to pray with absolute certainty that God would do **exactly** what He said He wanted to do.

As a result of getting guidance from God, Isaiah and Hezekiah **didn't doubt** that God would prevent the Assyrians conquering Jerusalem. The result of their trusting that God would do as He said is seen in 2 Kings 19:35-36:

"That night an angel of the Lord went to the Assyrian camp and killed 185,000 soldiers. At dawn the next day there they lay, all dead! Then the Assyrian

emperor Sennacherib withdrew and returned to Nine-
veh." (Good News Version)

When we read in the Scriptures about Peter, Paul, Elisha, or any believer praying for a miracle, we **should not wrongly assume** that just because the Scriptures don't give all the details about God showing them for what He wanted them to trust Him, that they didn't have some guidance from Him about this. For example, just because Elisha prayed for an axe handle, which was lost in a river, to surface (see 2 Kings 6:1-7), and he prayed for some poisonous food to no longer be poisonous (see 2 Kings 4:38-41), don't assume that God the Holy Spirit didn't guide him to trust Him to perform these miracles. The same applies to other miracles recorded in the Scriptures.

SHORT SUMMATION

All of the miracles recorded in the Scriptures, **except** for ones when God sovereignly did something without wanting people to exercise faith before He would do it, were prayed for in certainty only because the person had a promise from the Scripture to guide him, or had some guidance of the Holy Spirit on which to base his prayer.

The Holy Spirit will reveal the Father's will about what He wants us to trust Him to do by speaking a Word of the Lord to us.

In Luke 5:5, we see that Peter wouldn't let down his net to fish—he knew to catch fish there would have to be a miracle—unless God the Son told him to do so:

"And Simon answering said unto Him, 'Master, we have toiled all the night, and have taken nothing: nevertheless at THY WORD I will let down the net.'"
(Authorised Version)

We have to first get a Word of the Lord to reveal what God wants us to ask Him for, before we attempt to trust Him for a specific miracle.

15
God Has No Favourites

1 JOHN 3:21-22

Some Christians wrongly think that verses such as 1 John 3:21-22 and 1 Peter 3:7 suggest that we have to reach a special level of "holiness" or "worthiness" before God will answer our requests for miracles.

They misinterpret these verses. They do not interpret these verses in agreement with what other verses of Scripture say. We cannot say that one or a few Scriptures should be interpreted in a particular way, if this interpretation is contrary to the teachings of other Scriptures. The Bible must be **taken as a whole.**

Since we can see from other Scriptures that God performed miracles for men such as Moses, Paul and Elijah who **did not live totally good lives,** it is apparent that 1 John 3:21-22 is not suggesting that we have to never sin, for God to answer our requests for miracles. 1 John 3:21-22 really teaches that if we have sin in our lives that we have not confessed to God, asked His forgiveness for and repented of (turned away from), this sin will prevent us from having confidence before God in prayer. Confidence in prayer before God means having Biblical Holy-Spirit-inspired faith. As a result, Jesus Christ will mostly not allow His faith within us to be exercised towards the receiving of the miracle in answer to our prayer request.

Similarly, 1 Peter 3:7 teaches that sin which we have not confessed and of which we have not repented will hinder our prayers being answered by God.

1 John 3:21-22 could not possibly mean that a person would have to have never sinned, before God would answer his prayer request. No person except Jesus Christ has lived without sinning.

Once we confess and repent of our sins, 1 John 3:21-22 shows that we can be confident that God will answer our requests for miracles that are according to His will.

This is not to suggest that it is all right to sin deliberately. As the Apostle Paul in Romans 6:1-2 says:

"What shall we say, then? Should we continue to live in sin so that God's grace will increase? CERTAINLY NOT! We have died to sin—how then can we go on living in it?" (Good News Version)

It is very dangerous to sin deliberately because it may cause the sin itself and Satan to get such a hold on us that we will turn against God.

NO FAVOURITES

Many people think that God will only perform a miracle for them if they supposedly "earn" it by being good all of the time. They wrongly believe that God only performed or performs miracles for the Apostles, Prophets and those whom they regard as "holy Saints". They do not realize that **God has no favourites.** He loves Joshua, Elijah, Elisha, Moses, David, Mary, the Apostles Paul and Peter not one bit more than He loves you. If you don't know this, you don't really know God very much. You may have studied religion, theology or gone to church all of your life, but you don't really know His character. Romans 2:11 says:

"For God shows no partiality (undue favor, or unfairness; with Him one man is not different from another)." (Amplified Version)

This does not mean that we should deliberately disobey God, as Romans 6:1 shows.

Galatians 3:5 shows that God performs miracles for us as **free gifts** by our believing the gospel (Good News) about Jesus Christ and through having a personal love-trust relationship to Him. This verse says that God does not perform miracles for us by us being good by obeying the Law (the Commandments about not stealing, not killing, not lying, respecting our parents and so on that were given by God through Moses).

"Does God give you the Spirit and WORK MIRACLES among you because you do what the Law requires or

110

because you hear the gospel and believe it?"
                                    (Good News Version)

God wishes to perform miracles for us **not because we are good enough,** but **because He loves us totally** and because through the death and resurrection of Jesus Christ, He wishes to do this as part of deepening our personal love-trust relationship to Him.

God did not perform miracles for or answer the requests of the Apostles and Prophets **unless they asked for things that were His will.** Examples recorded in Mark 10:35-40 and Luke 9:53-56 prove this. These were discussed in Chapter 6. This shows that God did not do things for them that were His will, just because they supposedly "earnt" or "deserved" them due to some "special" level of holiness or obedience to Him that they were supposed to have had.

Why have the Apostles, Prophets and some dedicated Christians over the years had God perform more miracles for them than others? It is mostly that:

- they knew God's will about more things than do many other Christians because they had a greater desire to understand deeply the Scriptures and to recognize what the Holy Spirit wanted to say to them.
- they were more committed to allowing Jesus Christ within them to rule them and to seeing His Kingdom established more and more here on earth. This allowed Jesus to use them more easily—expressing His faith through them towards the things He knew and had revealed were the Father's will.

TOO UNWORTHY?

The people who say, "the Saints and holy men and women of years ago were worthy enough to receive miracles from God, but I'm not", have not read properly the historical records of the so-called "Saints" and holy men and women in all denominations. For every so-called "Saint" and holy person in the Catholic, Orthodox and various Protestant denominations over the centuries—Anthony of Padua, Francis of Assisi, Patrick (Apostle of Ireland), Luther, Calvin, Knox, Wesley, Carey, Whitefield, Spurgeon, Finney, John G. Lake and all others—sinned greatly in his/her life. **None of them were worthy enough by their human**

111

efforts alone for God to feel obliged to supposedly "reward" them with a miracle.

Some people may say, "I know that we don't have to be perfect for God to answer our requests for miracles. This is because no-one is perfect. But I believe that we have to reach a particular level of holiness and obedience to God before He will answer our requests for His miraculous intervention."

The problem with this statement though is **how holy** do we have to become before God will begin to miraculously intervene in our lives? Does He regard **one or two or three or four disobediences** a day as **the acceptable limit** before He will stop answering our requests for His miraculous intervention? Does He require 100 or 200 or 300 or 1000 or some other number of obediences to His will before He will regard us as worthy enough to receive answers to our requests for miracles? Such questions are **too ridiculous** to ask. The Scriptures do not give specific figures about the acceptable number of disobediences a day before He will supposedly stop answering our requests for miracles. Neither do they give any figures about a specific number of obediences to God's will that we have to perform each day before He will "reward" our so-called "worthiness" by answering our requests for miracles.

Nearly everyone with the above false understanding of why God performs miracles for us, usually thinks that they are not reaching their imagined standards of obedience that they think that God requires. This **false sense of unworthiness** is Satan-inspired and is one reason why thousands of church-goers feel that they cannot expect God to answer their requests for his miraculous intervention in their lives.

Only the Lord Jesus Christ was ever good enough to deserve to have God the Father perform miracles for Him. It is **foolish human pride** to imagine that we can ever be holy or "saintly" or worthy enough, for a perfect and totally holy God to have to reward our so-called "goodness".

God wants to perform miracles for us only because we have become His sons or daughters—by totally dedicating ourselves to Jesus Christ and by being born-again of the Holy Spirit. Because the Father sees Jesus Christ living within us, He sees us as being worthy of receiving His miracles.

The Father wants to perform miracles for us **because He loves us.** It has nothing to do with how "good" or supposedly "worthy" we are by human standards. James 5:17 shows this where it says that the Prophet Elijah had a **similar sinful unworthy nature** as we do, but God still answered his request for there to be no rain for three years in Israel. This verse says:

> *"Elijah was a man OF LIKE NATURE WITH OUR-SELVES and he prayed fervently that it might not rain, and for three years and six months it did not rain on the earth. Then he prayed again and the heaven gave rain, and the earth brought forth its fruit."*
>
> *(Revised Standard Version)*

Elijah was just as unworthy as we all are. He complained indirectly against God and wanted to die because he could not cope with Queen Jezebel's threats to kill him (see 1 Kings 19:4-18).

God performed great numbers of miracles for Moses, Elijah, Elisha and others in Old Testament times and for Peter, Paul and others in New Testament times, not because they were supposedly "good enough" or "worthy enough" for Him to do these things for them.

Moses was not worthy enough for God to answer His requests. He murdered a man (see Exodus 2:11-15). He disobeyed God about circumcising his son (see Exodus 4:24-26). He disobeyed God in the wilderness of Zin, resulting in God refusing to allow him to enter the Land of Canaan (see Numbers 20:1-13). Paul tortured and instigated and supported the murdering of Christians. He aimed to get them to reject Jesus Christ. He was not worthy enough for God to answer his requests for miracles. But God performed through these two men possibly more miracles than anyone else (see Deuteronomy 34:10-12, Acts 19:11-12).

The Lord Jesus said there had never been a man (except obviously Jesus Himself) who was greater in the Old Testament period than John the Baptist (see Matthew 11:11). Jesus was inferring that not even Elijah, Elisha, Moses or any so-called "Saint" was more supposedly "worthy" or "holy" than John the Baptist. But note that despite this, John 10:41 records that the Lord did no great miracle or sign through John the Baptist. This is further proof that God does not reward us with miracles in relation to our level of holiness or obedience to Him.

16
God Did Not Answer The Request Of The Most Humble Holy Person

An example in the Scriptures of God not answering the prayer request of someone who deeply knew and loved Him is seen in Deuteronomy 3:23-27. In this example, Moses asked God to allow him to cross the Jordan River and to go into the fertile land on the other side:

> *"At that time I earnestly prayed, 'Sovereign Lord, I know that you have shown me only the beginning of the great and wonderful things you are going to do. There is no god in heaven or on earth who can do the mighty things that you have done! Let me cross the Jordan River, Lord, and see the fertile land on the other side, the beautiful hill country and the Lebanon Mountains.' But because of you people the Lord was angry with me and would not listen. Instead, He said, 'That's enough! DON'T MENTION THIS AGAIN! Go to the peak of Mount Pisgah and look to the north and to the south, to the east and to the west. Look carefully at what you see, because YOU WILL NEVER GO ACROSS THE JORDAN....'"*
>
> *(Good News Version)*

God **did not answer Moses' prayer request.** The Lord told Moses that it was not His will for Moses in body to cross the Jordan River into the land of Canaan. (Later, after Moses' death, the Lord allowed Moses in spirit form to go to the land of Canaan—see Matthew 17:1-4.)

How foolish is the idea that God answers our prayer

requests on the basis of how holy, humble and obedient to His will we are! Numbers 12:3 reveals that Moses was the **most humble person** living on earth at that time:

> *"(Moses was a humble man, MORE HUMBLE THAN ANYONE ELSE on earth)."*   *(Good News Version)*

This means that Moses was the **most-dependent-upon-God** person living at his time. Moses had **stronger faith in God** than any person at the time. (Refer to the chapters "Pride" and "Humility" of my book, "KEYS TO KNOWING GOD BETTER—A Handbook About Holiness and Greater Dedication to God", for more details on how the Scriptures define the word "humility" and its opposite "pride".)

We may think that Moses was more worthy of having his prayer requests answered by God than what we are, but the Scriptures show that God did not answer those of his prayer requests that were not God's will.

God did not answer Moses' other prayer requests because of his great humility and obedience to God. As we will see in a later chapter, "Moses—A Great Example", God answered so many of Moses' other prayer requests because he prayed according to God's will.

In Deuteronomy 34:10-12, God reveals that He performed through Moses **more miracles** than any other prophet or "holy" person living until that time:

> *"There has never been a prophet in Israel like Moses; the Lord spoke with him face-to-face. No other prophet has ever done miracles and wonders like those that the Lord sent Moses to perform against the king of Egypt, his officials, and the entire country. No other prophet has been able to do the great and terrifying things that Moses did in the sight of all Israel."*
>
> *(Good News Version)*

God performed through Moses more miracles than any other person except the Lord Jesus and possibly the Apostle Paul (see Acts 19:11-12), possibly the other Apostles mentioned in the Bible (see Acts 5:12-16) and possibly Elijah and Elisha. It is likely that God performed through Moses far more amazing miracles than He did through Francis of Assisi, Anthony of Padua, Patrick of Ireland or any other so-called "Saint" or holy person.

If God refused to answer a prayer request of Moses

115

because it was not God's will, this shows that He would not answer a prayer request by one of these so-called "Saints" or other holy men if it were not His will. This is one reason why it is foolish for churchgoers to think by asking one of these so-called "Saints" to supposedly "intercede" to God for them, that their contrary-to-God's-will prayer request will be more likely to be heard than if they asked God directly themselves.

17
We Cannot Earn Miracles

Some books I've read give the impression that trusting God to perform miracles involves praying according to some **formula.** This is false.

Some Protestant authors I've read give the impression that we can **force** God to perform a miracle by positively thinking and/or speaking (called positively confessing) certain things, even though He has not revealed this miracle is His will. They suggest that if we keep thinking and/or saying that God is going to do a particular miracle, He will then have to do it. With little emphasis on finding God's specific will beforehand, others say that if we keep mentally picturing a specific miracle occurring (forming a vision of it in our minds), this will force God to perform the miracle. Others suggest that we can force God to perform a miracle if we keep acting as though God has granted our request. Many Pentecostals and Charismatics in the United States and elsewhere at the present time have been led by these Christian authors into these errors.

They make the exercising of faith into a **mere human effort works programme.** They think that they are **earning** an answer from God by their so-called "faith". We can never earn a miracle or force God to perform a miracle. This is because all miracles are **acts of God's grace.** The word "grace" in the New Testament is defined as a "gift" or "favour" or "benefit" or "kindness" that **cannot be earned** or **deserved,** no matter what we do.[1] They **are totally free.**

Romans Chapter 4 teaches a number of truths. But primarily, it is concerned with showing that Abraham was made righteous—made right with God—as a **totally free gift** of

God's **grace**—something that can **never be earned.** Romans 4:1-4 says:

> *"What shall we say, then, of Abraham, the father of our race? What was his experience? If he was put right with God by the things he did, he would have something to BOAST about—but not in God's sight. The scripture says, 'Abraham believed God, and because of his faith God accepted him as righteous.' A person who works is paid his wages, but they are not regarded as a GIFT; they are something that he has EARNED."*
> *(Good News Version)*

But note that the Apostle Paul in this chapter uses the example of Abraham trusting God to perform the **specific miracle** of giving him a son— even though he was 99 years old and Sarah, his wife was physically incapable of having a child—as part of his argument that we are accepted as being righteous by God as a **free unearned gift** received by faith. Since Paul refers to this specific miracle in this context, it is ridiculous to suggest that miracles such as these not specifically promised in the Scriptures can be "earned" by us in any way.

Romans 4:3,5,16 and 22 speak of Abraham and/or us being made righteous with God as a **result of faith.** But note as said above, the Apostle said in the same chapter that God has made it impossible to earn or deserve being made righteous and acceptable to God. This clearly reveals that **faith is not something which earns things from God.** It reveals that faith is instead the **means** by which we **accept humbly** many of the **free gifts** that God desires to give us. Faith is the hand that in enormous gratitude reaches out to receive **what God offers**.

When receiving Jesus Christ into our hearts as Lord and Saviour, we don't earn His presence and salvation by our faith. Our faith is instead the means by which we receive Him and His salvation in humility and with great thankfulness. Many born-again Christians do not realize that faith for miracles is very similar.

I've read some Christian books which suggest Genesis Chapters 15,17,18 and 21 and Hebrews 11:11 reveal that Abraham's faith earnt him the miracle of a son and many descendants. But such an interpretation is totally contrary to what Romans Chapter 4 says about faith and Abraham receiving God's free gift of righteousness and the specific miracle of a son.

The human race is full of pride. This is one reason why many of us— even as Christians—find it hard to understand how God will not allow us to earn or deserve anything— salvation, miracles, guidance and so on—from Him.

In Romans 4:2-4, the Apostle Paul reveals that if people could earn their salvation, they would be able **to boast.** This is another reason why God will not allow us to earn miracles supposedly by our "faith", prayer, fasting, human goodness or any other means. If we could earn miracles we could boast about how our faith is stronger than others, how much we pray and how good we are—forgetting miracles are undeserved free gifts.

As we shall see later, it is important to say, think and sometimes mentally picture what God wants us to, when trusting Him for a miracle. Also, as James 2:18-26 says, it is important to express our Holy Spirit-inspired faith in our actions. So don't think that I'm saying that these things are useless. But this is very different from thinking that we can force God to perform a miracle that is not His will, by often saying, thinking and mentally picturing or visualizing the miracle occurring.

INCORRECT USE OF PRAISE AND THANKSGIVING

Other Protestants I've heard suggest that if we just keep praising and thanking God enough, He will do whatever we ask. They usually don't stop to inquire if what they are asking is specifically God's will. They use praise and thanksgiving to God in a similar way that some husbands use flowers and other gifts to encourage their wives to do what they want.

The Scriptures are full of teaching about the great importance of praising God in **all** circumstances—good or bad (see Psalms 148-150, Acts 16:22-25). We are told to thank Him continually in every situation in our lives (see 1 Thessalonians 5:18). We are commanded to worship and praise Him for being the **sort of Person** and having **the sort of character** He has (see Psalms 95, 96, 117:1-4). It is also Scriptural to praise and thank Him that He is going to perform a specific miracle which He has revealed is His will. This praise is an expression of deep **confidence** and **trust** in Him.

But this is very different from trying to force God to perform a miracle that is not His will by praising, thanking and worshipping Him a lot. Praise, giving thanks and worship are not things to be used as magical formulas to try to earn miracles from Him, that He does not want to do. Nor are they to be used to try to get Him to change His mind about what His will is. They are **not "bunches of flowers"** that we send to Him to encourage Him to do what we want.

THE UNRIGHTEOUS JUDGE

Some Protestants and Catholics quote the example of the unrighteous judge (see Luke 18:1-8) to suggest that if we keep asking God in prayer for something **persistently** or **enough times,** this will **"earn"** for us a **reward**—an answer to our request—or this will somehow **force** Him in the end to give to us what we are asking, even if our request is contrary to His will. But such ideas are **contrary to the plain meaning of other verses of Scripture.**

The parable of the unrighteous judge was not told by the Lord Jesus to make us think that God the Father answers requests for miracles on the same basis as the unrighteous judge. The Father has a **totally different personality** from that of the unrighteous judge. The judge in the story shows no real love for the widow. He answers her request only so that she will stop bothering him and taking up his time. He helps her for his **own selfish reasons.**

God the Father's character is **totally opposite** to this. He does not regard our talking to Him to be a slightest bother. He loves us to talk to Him continually every day (see 1 Thessalonians 5:17). He would not regard a widow coming to Him for help as being a nuisance, because constantly in the Scriptures, He is seen to be very concerned about helping widows. This is seen in the words that He inspired the Scriptures' authors to write (see James 1:27, Isaiah 1:17, Psalm 146:9).

The Lord Jesus told this parable not to teach us to keep persistently asking the Father for something that is not His will, until He gets tired of us asking Him and He gives us what we ask to stop us pestering Him. Nor was Jesus teaching us that if we prayed for something persistently or enough times, this would earn for us an answer to our request from the Father.

Instead, as Luke 18:1 records, Jesus told the parable

of the unrighteous judge to encourage His disciples to never give up praying. Luke 18:7 infers that God is happy for His chosen children to cry out to Him day and night about any specific matter. This indicates that God is pleased for us to **pray persistently** to Him about the same matter often.

But note that the only types of persistence that Jesus is encouraging in Luke 18:1-8 are **a persistence in seeking to know God the Father's will** in the matter and/or **a persistence in faith**—a persevering, persistent, prayerful trusting in God to bring about what He has revealed is His will, no matter how long it takes to manifest and how impossible it seems of being fulfilled. In verse 8 of the parable, Jesus relates the importance of faith to this persistent praying.

Jesus was also teaching that if a selfish, unloving, unrighteous judge would answer a widow who kept asking him for something, HOW MUCH MORE would a totally loving, unselfish, righteous God desire to help us.

Proof of this is seen in Luke 18:7-8. Instead of saying that the Father will only answer us if we keep bothering Him enough by asking Him for the same thing enough times or if we supposedly "earn" an answer from Him by the number of times we pray, these verses say that He will answer His elect—His born-again sons and daughters—speedily. The unrighteous judge did not answer speedily.[2] For a period, he refused to answer (see verse 4). But these verses do not say that for any period, God refused to answer.

We **cannot take verses of Scripture in isolation.** We must take Luke 18:1-8 in relation to other Scriptures. Luke 11:5-13 has words in it very similar to Luke 18:1-8. It tells the story of a person whose friend gave to him what he asked because of his persistence in asking. But once again, it is not suggesting that God the Father is like the friend who gave. Instead, it infers that because a sinful human will help a friend because of the friend's persistence in asking, **how much more** will our totally unselfish, loving Heavenly Father want to help us. See also verses 11-13 where Jesus says that if a human father will give good things to his children who ask him, **how much more** than this does our Heavenly Father want to give us good things that are His will.

Luke 11:5-13 encourages us also to be persistent in our praying about specific matters. But when we take these verses **in context** with **surrounding verses** such as Luke 11:2 and its equivalent—Matthew 6:10, which emphasize asking

121

God for things that are His will and praying that God's rule—His Kingdom—shall be established over more and more things, we see that Jesus was encouraging persistent prayer based on these two things. Very often, as we persistently pray to Him about a specific matter, the more we commit our desires over to Him, the more He **changes** or **moulds these desires** until they come to be in agreement with His will. Then He gives us what we ask and seek for, as Jesus promised in the oft-quoted verses about asking and receiving, seeking and finding—Luke 11:9-10. Luke 11:1-13 cannot be fully understood if any of its parts are taken in isolation.

Many sermons have been preached over the centuries which take the parable of the unrighteous judge to teach things contrary to the rest of the teachings of the Scriptures. These sermons have made people wrongly think of God the Father as having a horrible character and have made many think that they have to almost force God to answer them.

The Father wants us to persistently pray to Him about problems we have, things we need and about everything else in our lives, not in order to try to earn an answer from Him or to try to force Him to answer us. He wants us to persistently pray to Him about these things, so we will learn:

- to communicate with Him about everything in our lives.
- to constantly see Him as the centre of our lives— the solver of our problems (see Psalm 23), the provider of our real needs (but not necessarily our wants), our greatest Friend Who wishes to share with us all of our good and bad times and the Person Who unselfishly loves us more than anyone else.
- to trust and rely on Him in all circumstances— good and bad. This trust and reliance in God in relation to a specific matter sometimes needs to be expressed **persistently** for **many months** or **years**.

Those who suggest that Luke 18:1-8 and Luke 11:5-13 are teaching that God will answer our prayer requests that are contrary to His will, if we are persistent enough and ask "enough" times, are arguing on a very shaky foundation.

In almost every instance, God only answers prayers that are His will (see 1 John 5:14-15). Those unaware of this are inferring that, if we like spoilt children, insist on our own way enough, God will always change His mind and give us something that we ask for that is not His will. This suggests that our persistence—in the Authorized Version "importunity" — will cause God to make His will about something subordinate to our own. This is very wrong.

As we saw in Chapter 9, "Asking Outside Of God's Will", the two clearest examples in the Scriptures of God answering requests that were not His will, reveal that enormous unnecessary troubles resulted for those who asked Him to do this. On both of these occasions, God did not answer their request just because they supposedly "earnt" an answer from Him by the number of times they had prayed.

If, however, Christians are aware that God in almost every instance only answers prayer requests based on His will, they are suggesting that we have to almost force Him to do things for us that are His will. What a **strange notion** this is! God desires to see His will occur in our lives **far more** than what we do ourselves. Many times, He desires to do things for us that we stubbornly will not allow Him to do. Matthew 23:37 reveals God's desires when talking of His attitude to the people of Jerusalem:

> *"Jerusalem, Jerusalem! You kill the prophets and stone the messengers God has sent you! How many times I wanted to put my arms around all your people, just as a hen gathers her chicks under her wings, but YOU WOULD NOT LET ME."*   (Good News Version)

God does not require us to be begging Him constantly to do the various aspects of His will in our lives. If you think that you have to beg Him, you do not know His character. Read Chapter 8 of my book, "KEYS TO KNOWING GOD BETTER". This chapter gives many details from the Scriptures of God's real and often misunderstood character. Could God say about you or me, "I wanted so much to help him, but **he would not let me**"?

The Lord Jesus' words in Matthew 6:7 reveal some very important things about prayer. He said:

> *"And when you pray do not (multiply words, repeating the same ones over and over, and) heap up phrases as the Gentiles do, for they think they WILL BE HEARD for their MUCH SPEAKING."*   (Amplified Version)

Here the Lord Jesus says that we should not pray like

the non-Israelite pagan nations—called the Gentiles—did. Jesus said that the members of these pagan religions thought that God would hear and answer their prayer requests if they kept praying these **enough times** or **prayed enough words.** The Lord Jesus' words could also be taken to include a criticism of the wrong attitude that God will reward us if He sees us praying a certain amount of times each day.

This does not mean that it is wrong to talk to God many times about the same problem. He likes us to **continually communicate with Him** about **everything** in our lives—asking Him for what we need, telling Him our problems, listening to His advice and guidance, trusting Him for His strength and help, telling Him how much we love Him and saying many other things. It is **tremendously important** that we pray as much as is possible.[3] We should aim to set apart **at least an hour** to **talk to** and **listen to** God each day. Throughout the rest of the day, at work or wherever, we should continue to pray little 30-second or one-minute prayers to keep in communication with Him.

God in 1 Thessalonians 5:17 commands us to pray continually throughout each day. God commands this so we can deepen the intimacy of our personal love relationship to Him. But this is different from trying to **earn** an answer from God to a request, by saying the same request over and over (**as though God is deaf or forgetful**) or by praying a number of memorised prayers over and over or by praying for a long time about other things.

I say the following in no way to draw attention to myself, but to teach you something. Over the years (especially between 1977 to 1981), I used to pray many times after work for 2 to 4 hours a night. This did not include praying on and off during the day. In my holidays and on weekends, sometimes I would pray for almost the whole day. This was not fleshly, formal repetitious prayers read out of books, but personal two-way communication with God. Occasionally, I would fast as well. On one occasion, I spent 24 hours straight in prayer, without sleep. These were tremendous times for me. They helped me grow to know and love God far more. But God revealed strongly to me during these times the Scriptural principle that He will not allow the amount of time we pray and/or fast or the number of times we ask for something, to "earn" a miraculous answer to any of our prayer requests. Instead, the Holy

Spirit revealed that as I opened myself to know His will and to allow His faith to inspire my prayer requests, I began to be able to trust Him to do miraculously the things He desired to do for me.

We cannot make it a rule, but mostly, assuming we pray with godly motives, the **more we pray:**

- the more we will know what miracles are His will.
- the more open we will be to receiving His faith which is needed to enable us to trust Him to perform these miracles.

These are two reasons why praying persistently is very important in attempting to trust God for miracles.

Church prayer meetings are very important (see Acts 4:23-31). But many are ineffective because people try to "earn" answers from God or boss Him, instead of seeking to pray according to His guidance and with His faith.

Thinking that the Father will hear and answer our prayer requests, if we pray these **enough times** or if we pray **a lot of words,** is what the pagan Gentiles do.

Many Hindus, Buddhists, Taoists and other pagans teach these attitudes to prayer that Jesus said were wrong. Many centuries ago, similar pagan attitudes infiltrated many Christian churches. They have been mixed with the teachings and practices of so many churches and many popular ministers, priests, bishops and so-called "Saints" that they are regarded wrongly as Christian Biblical notions.

This is when the matter of taking the Scriptures **as a whole** becomes important. We cannot take verses such as those about the unrighteous judge **in isolation** to suggest that we can earn answers from God or force Him to answer our contrary-to-His-will prayer requests by praying much, if other verses of Scripture teach differently from this idea. The Bible must be taken as a whole and not have its verses taken in isolation. Taking verses in isolation is like reading a newspaper article and then taking one sentence to mean something that is contrary to the rest of the words in the article.

OTHER FORMULAS

Many Roman Catholic and Orthodox Church members think that they can earn an answer from God by the number of times they pray the "Our Father" and other memorized prayers, the continual crossing of themselves in and out of church buildings, by helping the poor or doing social work, by fasting for a certain number of days, by having a particular number of holy communions, by holding particular religious rituals and so on.

None of these things will earn an answer to our request to God. It is very important to pray much, to occasionally fast, to participate in holy communion and to go to church. The Scriptures command us to *"Pray without ceasing"* (see 1 Thessalonians 5:17).[4]

If our attitudes are right when doing these things, the more we pray, go to church and so on, will help us in our praying for miracles because they will deepen the intimacy of our relationship to God. This in turn will make it easier for us to recognise what His Spirit wants us to pray and for our faith to be inspired and directed by Jesus within us towards the miracle or miracles that He wants to see occur. Matthew 17:20-21 infers this about prayer and faith.

Unconfessed, unrepented sins do the opposite. They hinder the Father from answering our prayer requests, by making us less sensitive to the guidance of the Holy Spirit and less controlled by the faith of Jesus living within us. Confession of sin and true repentance removes these hindrances.

However, no amount of prayer, fasting, participating in holy communion, going to church and doing anything else, will earn for us a miracle from God! We are **self-righteous** if we try to earn an answer from God by our own human attempts at being good.

FOOTNOTES:

1. James Strong, "EXHAUSTIVE CONCORDANCE OF THE BIBLE," Riverside Book and Bible House, Iowa Falls, P.417.

2. When saying that God will answer speedily, this does not necessarily mean that we will see the answer in the physical realm straight away. For as shown in the case of the prophet Daniel, God answered his request straight away, but the manifestation of God's answer did not occur until days after (see Daniel 10:1-14).

3. For more details about the exceptional importance of praying as much as is possible and how to do this in practice, refer to Chapter 28 "Prayer—Quality and Quantity" of my book "KEYS TO KNOWING GOD BETTER" and chapter 15 "Day to Day Practice of Seeking God's Will" of my book "HOW TO RECOGNIZE GOD'S VOICE."

4. Refer to Chapter 28, "Prayer—Quality and Quantity", in my book, "KEYS TO KNOWING GOD BETTER", for a detailed explanation of why we would pray.

18
James 5:16

Some Christian authors seem to suggest that the second part of James 5:16 is saying, "The **screaming, shouting** and/or **long** prayers of a **sinless** or **almost sinless** Christian will be answered by God, even if these requests are not specifically His will".

The word "fervent" in the original Greek is "zelos", which means "zeal, heat, fervent mind".[1] The word "effectual" in the original Greek is "energeo", which means "to be active, efficient, be mighty in, work (effectually in)."[2]

Because the words "fervent" and "effectual" have these meanings, some Christians infer that James 5:16 is saying that if we pray **loud enough** or **with enough human energy** or **emotion** or pray **for a long enough period of time,** God will supposedly reward us by giving us what we ask, even if this means **changing His will to fit in with our will.**

There is nothing wrong with praying loud or with much emotion or human energy. The Lord does not only like soft, whispering prayer. He does not look to see how loudly or softly we are praying. He looks instead at the **attitudes of our heart** when we are praying. Similarly, there is nothing wrong with praying for long periods of time. In fact, the Apostle Paul commanded us to pray as much as possible (see 1 Thessalonians 5:17).

But as Matthew 6:7 reveals, it depends on **our motives.** As previously stated, this verse shows that we are praying **like pagans do,** if we think that by the length of time we pray or the number of times we pray a specific prayer, we can force God to do something that is not His will or encourage Him to change His will to fit in with our limited goals.

James 5:16 says:

"...The effectual fervent prayer of a righteous man

availeth much."   *(Authorized Version)*

Some people wrongly take this verse out of context with surrounding verses and ignore other parts of the Bible by saying this verse means that we have to be **sinless,** or **almost sinless,** before our prayers will achieve much. We should take this verse in context with verses 17 to 18, commented on previously, and with the rest of verse 16 which talks of confessing our sins. Then we see that when James 5:16 is talking about a righteous man, it is referring to a person who:

- has a sinful human nature just like ourselves (see James 5:17), but
- has an **intimate personal love relationship** with God, and
- **constantly confesses** and **repents** of any sin that he may mistakenly get caught in (see James 5:16).

When we take the second part of James 5:16 in context with James 5:17-18, and in relation to a number of other Scriptures, our understanding of the second part of James 5:16 becomes clearer.

James in Chapter 5:17-18 goes on to give an illustration of what God regards as "the effectual, fervent prayer of a righteous man". James uses Elijah as an example of a righteous man (refer to my previous comments about how the Scriptures define what "a righteous man" is). James uses two of Elijah's prayer requests to God as examples of "fervent, effectual prayers". These are when Elijah trusted God to stop it raining for three and a half years and when at the end of these three and a half years, he trusted God to make it rain again.

If we cross-reference James 5:16-18 with 1 Kings 18:1, we see it was not the loudness or amount of human energy or emotion or the length of time that Elijah prayed that resulted in God performing these miracles, but because of **his zeal** in **seeking to pray only according to God's will** and **his effectual fervency** to **continue to trust God to do these things** that God revealed were His will. Such zeal and fervency obviously **outwardly expressed** itself in some form **of human emotion.**

1 Kings 18:1 does not say that God saw Elijah screaming and shouting enough loud prayers or saw him praying

for a long enough period for God to reward him by sending rain. Instead, it says:

"After some time, in the third year of the drought, THE LORD SAID to Elijah, 'Go and present yourself to King Ahab, and I will send rain'."

(Good News Version)

Elijah was zealously open to receiving God's guidance and then to fervently trust Him to do what He had revealed was His will.

Note in 1 Kings 18:28-29, we can see that it was the pagan Baal prophets who **shouted out loud** prayers to their demon-god. 1 Kings 18:26 shows that these Baal prophets also expressed **much fervency, human emotion** and **energy** while praying, but it was **not a fervency that pleased God.** This is because these Baal prophets had little fervency and zeal in seeking to know God's will, to intimately know and love Him and to trust Him to do only those miracles which were His will. Their effectual fervency was directed by them towards the demon-inspired practices of the evil Baal religion.

The Christian authors whom I mentioned misunderstand the second part of James 5:16, fail to realize that it is not just fervency, zeal, loudness and emotional prayer alone that results in God answering our prayer requests. It is **Holy Spirit-inspired** fervency and zeal directed towards finding God's will, in trusting Him to do those things that He shows are His will and in wanting to see His rule extend over more and more of our lives—and the lives of others.

FOOTNOTES:
1. Strong, op. cit., P.345.
2. Ibid, P.297.

19
What Is The Biblical Type Of Faith?

The Scriptures reveal many different aspects of what faith is. I have read some books which infer that faith in God relates mainly to receiving miracles from God. This is wrong. The Scriptures also show that faith in God relates to knowing God intimately, and trusting not in our strength and wisdom, but in His strength and wisdom. The Scriptures also show that faith is expressed by putting God **first**—glorifying Him—in everything we do, not making an idol of anyone or anything, aiming to please God instead of people, trusting God to forgive us and cleanse us of our sins and similar things. (Refer to my book, "KEYS TO KNOWING GOD BETTER", for much detail about these.)

I've spoken to some Catholics and Protestant Evangelicals who, when it comes to trusting God for miracles, define faith as though it is a mixture of knowledge and uncertainty. They seem to suggest that we can never be sure that God is going to answer our request for a specific miracle.

We can exercise faith in God in a **general sense,** while not knowing His will about everything in our lives. But it is impossible to exercise Biblical faith for a specific miracle from God unless:

- We know what His specific will is about the matter.
- We are expressing a **certainty** in our thoughts, actions and sometimes words that what He says is His will, He will do.

FAITH IS THE CERTAINTY

In Hebrews 11:1, God says, *"To have faith is to be SURE of the things we hope for, to be CERTAIN of the things we cannot see."* (Good News Version)

The Amplified Version of the Bible uses the word **"assurance"**. The word "assurance" means **"to be sure"**. The expression, "to be sure", means being certain. The Amplified says:

> *"Now faith is the ASSURANCE (the confirmation, the title deed) of the things [we] hope for, being the proof of things [we] do not see and the conviction of their reality—faith perceiving as real fact what is not revealed to the senses."*   *(Amplified Version)*

It is foolish to say that we are exercising faith for a specific miracle, when we are **not sure** that God will do as we ask. God Himself said, *"To have faith is to be SURE of the things that we hope for, to be CERTAIN of the things we cannot see."* If we are **sure** that God will give us the thing we have been hoping for, this is faith.

God **didn't** say that faith is the uncertainty or the state of not being sure that He will answer the prayer request in exactly the way that we are asking.[1] In Hebrews 11:1, God said that faith is the certainty of things that we cannot see.

If the Lord has revealed by His Spirit's guidance that it is His will to perform a particular miracle for us and we do not respond by being **sure** that we **will receive** this miracle, this is an **insult against God's character.** It is similar to you inviting someone to come to your place for a meal and this person getting down on his hands and knees, **begging** and **pleading** for you to feed him. This person's actions reveal he doubts whether you always do as you say, thereby inferring you are a **liar.** His actions reveal also that he doubts whether you love him enough to feed him. If the person really had faith in your character, he would be sure that he was going to receive from you what you stated you were going to do for him.

I'll say it again to help our minds to hear God's truth. Faith is the CERTAINTY. It is the ASSURANCE that we have the things that before we were only hoping to get.

For example, when Moses was trusting God to cause the Red Sea to part miraculously, the Scriptures do not say he was unsure that the miracle would happen. He was certain that it would happen (see Exodus 14:1-29, especially verses 13-27). But remember that this Biblical type of faith can be exercised only **after** we have found God's will first.

131

Moses didn't try to exercise faith for this miracle until after he had found out God's will (see Exodus 14:4, 15-18).

Faith is **not the state of being uncertain** that God will give us what we ask. This is why the "If it be Thy will" prayers of many churchgoers for miracles—falsely imagining that they are following the example of Jesus Christ in Luke 22:42—are not prayers of faith at all. (Refer to my booklet "MIRACLES—AND IF IT BE THY WILL" for details about Jesus' prayer in Luke 22:42. Many people misunderstand this prayer.)

When Paul, Peter, Philip and Stephen trusted God for miracles, were they unsure that the miracles would happen? No. Each knew that to trust God, they had to be certain that the miracle would occur.

The dictionary defines doubt as a **state of mind of being uncertain.** Therefore, if we try to pray for a miracle and we are uncertain that it is going to happen, we are praying with doubt. In His Holy Bible, God uses the word "doubt" in such verses as Matthew 21:21:

> *"Jesus answered, 'I assure you that if you BELIEVE and DO NOT DOUBT, you will be able to do what I have done to this fig-tree. And not only this, but you will even be able to say to this hill, "Get up and throw yourself in the sea", and it will'."*
>
> *(Good News Version)*

The word "believe" relates to faith, and since Hebrews 11:1 says, "Faith is the certainty", we see that doubt is uncertainty. If we are not certain that what we are wanting to ask God for is His will, we should not even attempt to trust Him for it, until we have studied the Scriptures and listened to His Holy Spirit's guidance to see if it is His will.[2] If we don't, we will pray a prayer full of doubt and uncertainty.[3]

PAGAN DEFINITION OF FAITH TAUGHT IN SOME CHURCHES

I've read some theological books which say that we can't be certain about anything. They call this "blind faith." This is not Biblical faith. It is merely the pagan philosophy of scepticism. Scepticism teaches that we can't be certain about anything.

Scepticism is a foolish philosophy because it teaches a

logical contradiction. It really says, "I am **certain** that we **can't be certain** about anything." How can we be certain about one thing and then in the next breath say that we can't be certain about anything? This is a contradiction. Philosophers and church leaders who teach such nonsense are deceived by their own limited human wisdom (see 1 Corinthians 1:19-29, 2:1-13, Colossians 2:8 and 1 Timothy 6:20-21).

Some church leaders teach a **sugar-coated form of scepticism** about prayer, miracles and faith. They are not sceptical that God exists. But they teach pagan, sceptical philosophical ideas about other matters in a way that deceives churchgoers. They do this by using Biblical notions such as "faith", "God's will "and" submission to God's will" in ways which God didn't originally use when He guided the authors of the Scriptures what to write. For example, some church leaders say that praying in faith for a miracle involves not knowing God's will about if He wants to perform the miracle, and then **blindly** saying, "Lord, if this is Your will, do so and so...for me." With a **pagan attitude** of **fate**, they then look at their circumstances to see if God has done what they asked. If it appears He has, they say it is God's will. If it appears He has not, they say it is not His will. They think that this is "submission to God's will." It is not. True submission is seeking to know God's will from the Bible and His Holy Spirit and then trusting Him to do what He says He wants to do in our lives. True submission involves also doing what is written in Chapter 22 "When We Don't Know His Will."

The Scriptures teach that faith is being **just as certain** that God will perform a miracle, for example, raise a friend from the dead (after His Spirit has shown us He wants to do this) as we are that our house or car exists. This is **Biblical faith** in relation to praying for **specific** miracles.

TRUE FAITH

Faith for miracles is associated mostly with aiming to trust God for miracles that are His will, and being certain that we will get what we trust Him for, as seen in 1 John 5:14-15.

As is shown in my booklet, "MIRACLES—AND IF IT BE THY WILL", 1 John 5:14-15 is not talking about the common misinterpretation of Jesus' "If it be Thy will" prayer recorded in Luke 22:42, because that misinterpretation is not based on assurance that we will get what we request.

God inspired the Apostle John to use similar words about having our prayer requests answered to those He used in Hebrews 11:1 to define "faith". In the Amplified Version of 1 John 5:14, the words **"assurance"** and **"sure"** are used about the result of any prayer based on God's will. 1 John 5:15 uses similar expressions. It says that we can have "**a settled and absolute knowledge**"—a certainty in our minds—that God has "granted us as our **present possession**" the thing for which we have asked Him. But we must make sure, before asking, that our prayer will be based on God's will as revealed in the Holy Scriptures or by the guidance of His Holy Spirit.

We should meditate on 1 John 5:14-15 until our mind fully understands these verses. Our natural mind, without meditation on these Scriptures and without the Holy Spirit revealing these Scriptures to us, will find it very hard to understand their meaning.

Romans 10:17 and John 15:7 also relate closely to 1 John 5:14-15 and Hebrews 11:1. Unless we understand them all, we will not understand how to pray in faith for specific miracles.

It is impossible to pray in agreement with Hebrews 11:1, if we are praying in terms of the common misinterpretation of Jesus' "If it be Thy will" prayer. This is because when we are praying "If it be Thy will", we are not sure that God will give us the thing that we are hoping to receive and will not be certain that He will give us something that we presently can't see with our eyes. For example, if we are praying for an 89-year-old woman to have a baby and we add to our prayer, "Lord, do this if it be Thy will," then we are obviously **not sure** that God is going to give us **the thing**—the baby—that we have been **hoping for.** Also, we are **not certain** that God is going to give us **the thing**—the baby—that we at present **can't see** with our eyes. Therefore, according to Hebrews 11:1, we are not praying in faith. Hebrews 11:1 says:

"To have faith is to be SURE of THE THINGS we HOPE FOR, to be CERTAIN of THE THINGS we CANNOT SEE."   (Good News Version)

134

Compare the wording of Hebrews 11:1 to the wording of my example above! After comparing the two, can you now see that the above example of prayer can never be a prayer of faith?

Many churchgoers have been wrongly taught that faith is some kind of "airy fairy" thing in which we believe that something exists, or something will occur even though we can never be sure that the thing exists or that the thing will occur. This is not what God in the Bible teaches that faith is. Many just accept what they are taught in their local church, without checking to see if God teaches the same in the Bible.

UNCERTAINTY EQUALS DOUBT

In relation to trusting God for specific miracles, the words "to be certain" are defined as the state of having no doubt that what we are believing God for will definitely come to pass.

UNCERTAINTY EQUALS DOUBT. Not being sure that our prayer request will be answered equals doubting. Doubt is sin.

Being tempted to doubt God, His character and what He tells us **is not sin**. Giving in to this temptation—allowing this doubt in God to control our minds—is sin. When trying to trust God for a miracle that is His will, often our minds will be tempted by doubts originating in **our own minds** or **from demons.**

Doubt is only a sin when it is directed **towards God.** It is not sinful for us to doubt that what another human is telling us is true. We would be fools if we believed everything another human says. Every human has only part knowledge. Humans also lie sometimes.

James 1:6-8 uses the word "wavering" in most versions of the Scriptures. In the original Greek, the word "wavering" comes from the word "diakrino" which means doubting. The Amplified Version brings out the result of us not being certain that God will give us exactly what we ask:

"Only it must be in faith that he asks, with no wavering—no hesitating, no doubting. For the one who wavers (hesitates, doubts) is like the billowing surge out at sea, that is blown hither and thither and tossed by the wind. For truly, let not such a person imagine that he will receive anything [he asks for] from the

135

Lord, [For being as he is] a man of two minds— hesitating, dubious, irresolute—[he is] unstable and unreliable and UNCERTAIN about everything (he thinks, feels, decides)."

If we are uncertain that God will give us what we ask when this thing is specifically His will for us, this is doubting. This will stop us from receiving God's answer to our prayer request, unless He acts in His sovereign love and mercy alone—as explained in Chapter 21, "The Sovereignty of God."

Since faith in relation to praying for specific miracles is certainty (see Hebrews 11:1), substitute the word "certainty" in verse 6 and the word "uncertainty" for doubting and see the result. It's incredible! It would read, "Only it must be in CERTAINTY that he asks, with NO UNCERTAINTY at all. For the one who is uncertain is like the billowing...". Substitute the words "is certain" for the word "believe" and the words "is uncertain" for the word "doubt" in verses such as Mark 11:23-24 and then relate them to 1 John 5:14-15 and Romans 10:17 and see how your understanding of these verses increases also.

80-90 YEAR-OLD LADIES HAVING BABIES

We may be saying again at this point. "How can I be certain that if I prayed for an 89-year-old woman, who is past child-bearing age, to have a child, that God would answer?" The answer to this question is that we could only be sure God would answer this prayer request if He spoke through the inner guidance of His Holy Spirit, telling us that it is His will that we should believe that this 89-year-old woman would have a child. As Romans 10:17 says in paraphrased form, "Faith comes by hearing the Word of the Lord." This is the only means by which we will be able to have Biblical, Holy Spirit-inspired faith to pray with certainty.

John 15:7 infers that once we have the Word of the Lord about a matter, we can be sure that what we ask of God will come to pass. This verse says in the Amplified Version:

"If you live in Me—abide vitally united to Me—and MY WORDS remain in you and CONTINUE to live

in your hearts, ask whatever you will and it SHALL be done for you."

The Lord Jesus in this verse uses the word "shall". This word "shall" is used in the sense of saying that a person who is born again and asks for what God reveals is His will, will certainly get the thing promised to him by this Word of the Lord. This verse does not say **possibly** or **maybe** this will happen.

Is it ridiculous trying to pray with certainty that an 89-year-old woman could have a child? If we say this, this shows that we know little of what the Scriptures teach. For this is what Abraham trusted God to do for his wife. His wife was 89 years old and had stopped having her monthly periods, when God told Abraham that she would have a son (see Genesis 17:1-21, especially verses 17 and 21, and Romans 4:19). Abraham prayed with certainty that God was going to give her a child (see Romans 4:19). He didn't pray in terms of the common misinterpretation of Jesus' "If it be Thy will" prayer. He was not uncertain that God would do exactly as he was asking. According to the principles spoken of in Hebrews 11:1, Abraham was sure of the thing that he hoped for—the hope that his 89-year-old wife would have a baby son—and was certain of the thing that he didn't see with his human eyes—he couldn't see with his human eyes for about one year the son that God had promised him.

After praying in certainty for about one year, Abraham saw Sarah have a baby at the age of 90 years (see Genesis 17:17,21).[4]

Abraham knew that first he had to learn God's will. He was sensitive to God's voice. Then after hearing what God's will was, he had a certain attitude that his very old wife would miraculously have a son.

FOOTNOTES:

1. As stated in Chapter 17, we can never earn a miracle by what we do. So by being certain that the miracle will occur, we **are not earning** its occurrence from God. When we are certain the miracle will occur, we are merely allowing our thoughts, words and actions to **co-operate with** and **express** the certain faith that Jesus Christ within us has towards the specific miracles the Father wants to do.

2. Study Chapter 22, "When We Don't Know His Will", to see what we should do if the Scriptures don't reveal His will about the matter and if the Holy Spirit has not given us clear guidance of the Father's will as yet.

What Is The Biblical Type Of Faith?

3. Many times when we begin to reach out to God for a specific miracle, many thoughts of doubt will come into our mind about whether God will do for us what He has said is His will. If we **resist** these doubts, we will find that Holy Spirit-inspired faith will take more and more control of our minds, and then our words and actions. A calm, peaceful, God-inspired assurance will take possession of our minds, the more we **discipline our thoughts** to not accept these doubts. As stated in Chapter 17, "We Cannot Earn Miracles", this will not earn us a miracle from God. But it will achieve His purpose in training us to trust in Him more than before. God will bless us by giving us this **free gift** of a miracle **at the time that He knows is best for us.** Do not be worried if you are having to fight many doubts about God doing what He has shown you is His will. This is part of the testing of your faith (see 1 Peter 1:6-7).

4. When we take Genesis 17:18 and 17:21 together, it seems that it was only in the last twelve months before the birth of Isaac that Abraham knew that it was God's will for the promised son to come through Sarah. Up until this time, it seems that Abraham thought that Ishmael—his son through Sarah's slave girl—was the promised son. Genesis 17:1, 17:17 and Romans 4:19, when taken together, show that after God had revealed His will about Sarah, Abraham trusted God to produce his son through her, even though he was 99 years of age, and she was 89 years and physically incapable of having children. Years before this, when first God told Abraham he would be given a son (see Genesis 12:2, 13:14 and 15:1-16), but did not reveal it would be through Sarah, Abraham trusted God to give him a son —but not specifically through Sarah. Because he was influenced wrongly by one of the pagan customs of the time, Abraham thought previously that God may have given him the son through his wife's slave girl.

20
Faith Response

Some people ask that if it is God's will for Him to perform specific miracles for us, why do we have first to find God's will and then have to believe with certainty that what God shows is His will, will come to pass? They may think, "If God is all-powerful, if it is His will, He doesn't need us to believe with certainty that it will happen, before it will happen." They don't understand parts of the Scriptures.

In His Holy Scriptures, God shows that He Himself has decided to limit **some** (but not all) of the manifestations of His miracle-working power to the degree that we allow Holy Spirit-inspired faith to control us and be expressed through our minds and spirits. Who am I to argue with God, if He has decided to limit Himself in this way? It is not people who have decided to limit God to this. No, God Himself has decided to do it. So God's sovereignty **is still unchallenged**.

Evidence of God sovereignly deciding to limit Himself in some instances is, even though in Jeremiah 25:11 and 29:10 God said that it was His perfect will that after being captives in Babylon for many years, the Jews were to return to Jerusalem and rebuild their nation, God didn't perform this miracle until people such as Daniel prayed with assurance that the miracle was going to occur (see Daniel 9:1-27). If God did not require someone to trust Him prayerfully to do this miracle, why did the angel in Daniel 10:12 say that God had heard Daniel's prayer and that the angel had come **in response** to this prayer?

Nehemiah also prayed for God's will to be brought about in this matter (see Nehemiah 1:1-11). Nehemiah didn't just sit back and say, "Well, it's God's will that the Jews who have returned from Babylonia rebuild Jerusalem and the nation, so there is little use in me praying that this occurs. God doesn't require me or anyone else to pray in faith that His will, as revealed in the Books of Moses in the Scriptures, must occur." Instead, Nehemiah prayed, trusting God to do exactly as He had promised Moses He would do. Nehemiah would have been wasting his time praying if God did not want him to do it.

Daniel found God's will in Jeremiah, and Nehemiah found God's will in the writings of Moses (see Nehemiah 1:7-9). Nehemiah was not only used by God to pray for the Lord's will to be manifested. He also was used by God in his actions to bring about the Lord's will.

Matthew 13:58 is a verse of Scripture which shows that God has sovereignly decided on many occasions to limit His performance of miracles to whether a person or people praying are exercising faith—being certain that the miracle will occur. This verse says:

> *"BECAUSE they DID NOT HAVE FAITH, He did not perform many miracles there."*
>
> *(Good News Version)*

This verse uses the word "because" which is a word used to show that there is a **relationship** between the amount of Holy Spirit-inspired faith (or certainty) expressed and the number of miracles that the Lord will perform. In Matthew 17:20, the Lord Jesus said that lack of faith prevented the Apostles from casting out a demon.

If God doesn't require this attitude of faith before He will perform many miracles, why then does Hebrews 11:11 say:

> *"It was FAITH that MADE Abraham ABLE to become a father, even though he was too old and Sarah herself could not have children."?*
>
> *(Good News Version)*

Why does Hebrews 11:29 say:

> *"It was FAITH that MADE the Israelites ABLE to cross the Red Sea as if on dry land..."?*
>
> *(Good News Version)*

Why does Hebrews 11:30 say:

> *"It was FAITH that made the walls of Jericho fall down*

after the Israelites had marched around them for seven days."?   *(Good News Version)*

Why does Matthew 9:2 say that when the Lord Jesus saw the **faith** of the paralysed man and of the men who brought him to Jesus that He healed the man?[1]

Why does the Lord Jesus in Matthew 9:22 say:

"Your FAITH has made you well",
      (Good News Version)

to the woman who was just healed of an issue of blood?

Why does Matthew 9:28 say that Jesus tested the **faith** of the two blind men who came to Him wanting to be healed, by saying:

"Do you believe that I can heal you?"
      (Good News Version)

In the Amplified Version, verse 29 states that Jesus said to the two blind men:

"According to your FAITH and trust and reliance [on the power invested in Me] be it done to you."

Why does the Lord Jesus in Matthew 14:31 infer that Peter began to sink because of his lack of **faith**, doubting and uncertainty?

Why does Jesus say in Matthew 15:28 that as a result of the Canaanite woman's **faith** that He would cast the demon out of her daughter?

Why does Jesus say in Mark 10:52 to the previously blind Bartimaeus:

"Your FAITH has made you well."?
      (Good News Version)

Why does Jesus in Luke 5:20-26, 7:9-10 and 8:48 say that miracles occurred as a result of their **faith**?

Why does the Lord Jesus in Luke 17:19 say to the man who previously had leprosy:

"Your FAITH has made you well."?
      (Good News Version)

And why does Acts 3:16 and Acts 14:9 say that **faith** resulted in God performing miracles?

In each of the above historical events recorded in the Scriptures, the people exercising faith for the miracles didn't say to themselves such things as, "**I wonder** if God is going to perform this miracle that He has promised in His Word or promised through Jesus' mouth or through the revelation of the Holy Spirit? I'm **not really sure** it is going to happen. I hope the miracle will happen, but **I can't be certain.**" Attitudes such as these would be, according to Hebrews 11:1 and 1 John 5:14-15, expressions of doubt and little faith.

At this point, you may be saying that it is **God** and **not faith** that performs miracles. This **is true**. But the point is that God in His great wisdom has apparently decided to limit His performance of miracles among humans in **many** cases to whether those who have God's will revealed to them from the Scriptures and/or from the inner guidance of God's Spirit, respond in faith, or if they respond in uncertainty and doubt.

There have probably been some things in our lives that God has wanted to do for us. But He has not done these things, because we did not in assured faith ask Him to do these things when He was (via His Scriptures or Holy Spirit) trying to show us that He wanted to do these things for us.

FOOTNOTE:

1. As stated previously, this book is not about healing miracles. But these verses are quoted to show the importance of faith response in many situations.

21
The Sovereignty Of God

Over the years, some Christians have argued that God will not do things in His physical creation and in the affairs of believers unless:

- some person prays to Him **asking** Him to do these things, and/or
- some person **exercises faith–trusting** Him to do these things.

The above statements are true in **some** circumstances, but not in all situations.

God miraculously made the universe and the human race without any person asking or trusting Him to do so (see Genesis Chapters 1 and 2).

God oversees the affairs of the birds without any person asking or trusting Him to do so. Matthew 10:29 says:

"For only a penny you can buy two sparrows, yet not one sparrow falls to the ground without your Father's consent."   (Good News Version)

Matthew 6:26 says:

"Look at the birds flying around: they do not plant seeds, gather a harvest and put it in barns; yet your FATHER IN HEAVEN TAKES CARE OF THEM!..."
      (Good News Version)

God makes flowers beautiful and clothes the grass without any person asking or trusting Him to do so. Matthew 6:28-30 shows this:

"Look how the wild flowers grow: they do not work or make clothes for themselves. But I tell you that not even King Solomon with all his wealth had clothes as

beautiful as one of these flowers. It is God who clothes the wild grass—grass that is here today and gone tomorrow, burned up in the oven......" (Good News Version)

The Scriptures reveal that on most occasions, God sends rain whether or not people ask Him or trust Him to do so. Matthew 5:45 says in part:

"...For he makes his sun to shine on bad and good people alike, and gives rain to those who do good and to those who do evil."   (Good News Version)

This verse also says that He makes the Sun shine on people. He does this without any person asking or trusting Him to do so.

Acts 14:17 says about God:

"But he has always given evidence of his existence by the good things he does: he gives you rain from heaven and crops at the right times..."   (Good News Version)

The Scriptures reveal that only on some occasions does God require humans to ask or trust Him to restore or stop the rainfall. Revelation 11:6, 1 Kings 17:1, 18:1 and James 5:17-18 reveal this. So does 2 Chronicles 7:13-14:

"Whenever I hold back the rain or send locusts to eat up the crops or send an epidemic on my people, if they pray to me and repent and turn away from the evil they have been doing, then I will hear them in heaven, forgive their sins, and make their land prosperous again."   (Good News Version)

Note this verse reveals that when God holds back the rain, He not only requires people to pray to Him asking Him to increase the rain. He also requires all or at least many of them to **turn from their sins.**

Job 1:8-19 reveals that God **sometimes allows** Satan to have influence over the lightning, storms and the rain. However, the Scriptures show that mostly God Himself controls the rainfall and other aspects of the weather.

I have heard some Christians suggest that God cannot do anything in the Universe or for believers unless they ask Him or trust Him to do so. Their supposed reason for this is the suggestion that since the fall of Adam and Eve, Satan legally owns the universe, the earth and the human race. They say that verses such as Matthew 4:8-9 and John 14:30

prove this, in that these verses say that Satan is the ruler of this world.

Such Christians make a **very simple mistake.** They do not realise that when the New Testament says that Satan is the ruler of this world, it is not suggesting that Satan is the ruler of God's physical creation —the rain, Sun, winds, oceans, rivers, mountains, trees, animals, birds, insects and other natural things.[1] The Biblical expression, "the world", in the original Greek of the New Testament refers to the **pressuring system** that tries to influence us to think in ways contrary to God's will as revealed in His Scriptures and by His Spirit.[2] It is the **non-Christian way** of **thinking** and **acting** that constantly uses other people, advertising, television, even many religious ideas and practices and many other things to try to get us to conform to it.

John 16:11 says of Satan's rulership of "the world":

"...because the ruler of this WORLD has been already judged."   (Good News Version)

John 14:30 says a similar thing. 1 John 5:19 says:

"We know that we belong to God even though the WHOLE WORLD is under the RULE of the EVIL ONE."   (Good News Version)

The fall of Adam and Eve did not hand over control of God's natural creation to Satan. Satan is not in control of the weather, even though, as said before, God may occasionally allow him to influence it. God still owns His physical creation. Psalm 50:9-11 says:

"And yet I do not need bulls from your farms or goats from your flocks; all the animals in the forest are MINE and the cattle on thousands of hills. All the wild birds are MINE and all living things in the fields."
          (Good News Version)

These words were spoken years **before** the Lord Jesus died on the Cross and was later resurrected. So even in Old Testament times, God still owned the physical creation. 1 Corinthians 10:26 speaks similarly:

"For, as the Scripture says, 'The EARTH and EVERY-THING IN IT belong to THE LORD'."
          (Good News Version)

145

Luke 10:21 says that God the Father is still the Lord of the physical Earth:

"At that time Jesus was filled with joy by the Holy Spirit and said, 'Father, LORD of heaven and EARTH...'."　　　　　　　　*(Good News Version)*

The fall of Adam and Eve put the human race into the hands of Satan. 2 Timothy 2:26 and Ephesians 2:1-2 infer this. Ephesians 2:1-2 says:

"In the past you were spiritually dead because of your disobedience and sins. At that time you followed the world's evil way; you obeyed the RULER of the spiritual powers in space, the spirit who now controls the people who disobey God."　　　　*(Good News Version)*

However, the Scriptures reveal clearly that after the Lord Jesus' death and resurrection, any person, who becomes born-again, no longer is a member of what the Scriptures call "the world." Galatians 6:14 says:

"But far be it from me to glory (in anything or any one) except in the cross of our Lord Jesus Christ, the Messiah, through Whom the world has been crucified to me, and I to the world."　　　　*(Amplified Version)*

Colossians 2:20 says a similar thing:

"If then you have died with Christ to material ways of looking at things and have escaped from the WORLD'S crude and elemental notions and teachings of externalism, why do you live AS IF YOU STILL BELONG TO THE WORLD?...."　　　　*(Amplified Version)*

Born-again Christians are **in** the world, because they must live and work among non-Christians (see Philippians 2:15, 1 Peter 5:9) who are a part of the world system ruled indirectly or directly by Satan and his demons. But Christians are **not of** the world—they are not members of the non-Christian world system. Instead, they are members of God's Kingdom (see Colossians 1:13). Therefore, sovereignly, God can perform miracles for them even if they do not ask or trust Him to do so.

The Scriptures also reveal that before the Lord Jesus' death and resurrection, God did things miraculously in the lives of those who loved and knew Him, even when they did not ask or trust Him to do so. This is despite their great weaknesses and sinful nature—see James 5:17. An example of this is recorded in Genesis 19:16. This is when sovereignly, the Lord told His two angels to take Lot, his wife and two daughters by the hand to get them out of Sodom to save their lives. The Lord did this even though Lot hesitated about going.

A second example of this is recorded in Genesis 20:1-9. Here, sovereignly, God helped Abraham and Sarah to get out of the awful mess that Abraham's partial lying had gotten them into. God helped them even though neither of them asked or trusted Him to do so.

A third example is seen in Genesis 19:1-11. In these verses, we observe that neither Lot nor anyone else asked or trusted God to have his two angels pull Lot back to safety inside his house when the homosexual men threatened him. Neither did Lot or anyone else ask or trust God to have his angels strike with blindness these homosexuals. The last three sections of this chapter of my book provide three other examples of God helping believers sovereignly before Jesus Christ's death and resurrection. These believers asked Him to help them but did not have faith for Him to do so.

GOD INFLUENCING UNBELIEVERS

God always acts with **perfect justice** in **all** circumstances towards every human, angel or demon. Humans have been given a free-will. By their own free-will choice, Adam and Eve rejected God's rule over their lives. They preferred to be self-reliant, independent-from-God beings. Since Satan and his demons are self-sufficient and independent from God also, Adam and Eve made themselves knowingly or unknowingly a part of Satan's kingdom. Without God, Adam and Eve were no match for Satan in power or intelligence.

As a result of what Adam and Eve did, every human descendant of theirs has been born in a state of having no personal relationship with God. They are born self-sufficient and without the presence of the Holy Spirit within them.

Many humans may choose to remain in this state of having no personal love-trust-dependence relationship to God. If they choose this, it is possible that God would not be acting in perfect justice towards them and Satan if He used His infinite power to influence them towards becoming a Christian, unless some Christian asked or trusted Him to do so.

Verses such as Ezekiel 22:20-31 seem to confirm this. Also, verses such as 1 Timothy 2:1-2, Romans 10:1 and 12:14 which speak of the importance of praying for unbelievers, seem to hint at this.

To what degree God has stated that He cannot influence unbelievers because of the above reasons, I am unsure. This is because in Genesis 11:1-9, it is recorded that God did things that greatly affected the lives of many unbelievers at the tower of Babel. But note, this had nothing to do directly with their salvation.

Whatever the case, it is very important for Christians to ask and trust God to minister to specific unbelievers by Him convicting them of their sin of rejecting Jesus as their Lord and Saviour (see John 16:8) and so on.

God has not decided to allow the fall of Adam and Eve to determine that He will only intervene in the affairs of His natural creation—rain, Sun, trees, birds and so on—if some person asks or trusts Him to do so.

God is **totally sovereign.** So He can do whatever He likes. He **does not need a push** from what I've heard some call "the force of faith". God is **infinitely powerful.** He has power to do anything without the **microscopic** assistance of our faith or prayers.

REASONS WHY GOD REQUIRES A FAITH RESPONSE SOMETIMES

But we must remember that in many instances, He waits until we trust Him to do something (that He has revealed is His will), before He will miraculously move on our behalf. One of the reasons why He does this, is that this **teaches us** to train our minds **to trust more and more in His love** and **power** and **to rely more and more on Him living within us.**

Also, if He always performed miracles without first revealing that they are His will and secondly having us focus ourselves on trusting Him to do these things, we would very likely not realise that He was the One Who had done these things for us. We would possibly think that these things were coincidences or luck or events caused merely by so-called "Mother Nature".

BALANCE BETWEEN GOD'S SOVEREIGNTY AND HUMAN FAITH RESPONSE

When considering the Sovereignty of God, we need to

be careful that we do not begin to have a **hyper-Calvinistic over-emphasis** on the place of God's Sovereignty in His performance of miracles. Such an over-emphasis is when we begin to think that **every** miracle is performed by God with no concern by Him about human faith response. Such an over-emphasis is clearly unscriptural as shown by such chapters as "What Is The Biblical Type of Faith?", "Faith Response", and others.

Hyper-Calvinism is an extreme interpretation of the teachings of John Calvin, one of the godly early 16th century Protestant leaders. Hyper-Calvinism teaches that God predetermines every event in the Universe—including His performance of miracles— and thereby ignores any human responsibility in praying for or trusting Him for these things. Hyper-Calvinism is very similar to pagan **fate** teachings.

Some churchgoers over-emphasise the place of human responsibility for exercising faith in God for Him to do something. Others over-emphasise God's sovereignty in His performance of miracles.

The Holy Scriptures emphasise **both** the Sovereignty of God and human responsibility to exercise faith in some situations when God performs miracles. If we ignore either Scriptural teaching, we will become **unbalanced** in our walk with God.[3]

ZECHARIAH AND ELIZABETH

In Luke 1:5-25, we see recorded an example of God **in mercy** performing a miracle for someone even though the person **did not trust God to perform this miracle.** This example relates to Zechariah, who was to become the father of John the Baptist.

Zechariah and his wife, Elizabeth, had never had a child. However, as we can observe in verse 13, Zechariah had **prayed** to God, asking Him to give them a child. It is not clear in this verse or surrounding verses whether he had been asking God for a child or specifically for a boy.

As recorded in verse 13, the angel Gabriel told Zechariah that it was God's will for his prayer request to be answered. Gabriel added that this God-given son would be the fulfillment of prophetic predictions that God had spoken through the prophets Malachi and Isaiah (see Luke 1:16-17 and compare to Malachi 4:5-6 and Isaiah 40:3).

Zechariah's response to these revelations of God's will

through the angel was **not a faith response** such as given by Abraham when Abraham was told by God that God was going to give him a son and many descendants. As seen in Romans 4:18-21, Abraham totally trusted God to perform the miracle of giving him a son through his wife Sarah. Abraham trusted God to do this even though Sarah was physically too old to have children. But Zechariah said:

"How shall I know if this is so? I am an old man, and my wife is old also." (Luke 1:18, Good News Version)

This verse and Luke 1:7 reveal that both Zechariah and Elizabeth were old as well. It is not clear whether they were as old as Abraham and Sarah or not. But whatever the case, we can see from the angel Gabriel's words that Zechariah doubted **the Word of the Lord**—the revelation of God's will spoken by the angel. Luke 1:19-20 says:

"'I am Gabriel', the angel answered. 'I stand in the presence of God, who sent me to speak to you and tell you this good news. But YOU HAVE NOT BELIEVED my message, which WILL COME TRUE at the right time. Because you HAVE NOT BELIEVED, you will be unable to speak; you will remain silent until the day my PROMISE to you comes true'."   *(Good News Version)*

Gabriel said that Zechariah did not believe what God had told Gabriel to tell Zechariah. As seen in Luke 1:18, Zechariah allowed his natural mind to focus so much on the **seeming impossibility** of his physical circumstances—the old age of himself and his wife— that he could not trust God to do the miracle for him that God had promised. Even though Zechariah was **a priest** (see Luke 1:5) and **righteous in God's sight** (see Luke 1:6), he had not learnt from Abraham's example I've quoted above.

Despite this lack of believing, still God gave Zechariah the promised son. As Luke 1:58 says, God still acted with **mercy—unearned favour** and **kindness**—towards Zechariah's wife, Elizabeth:

"And her neighbours and relatives heard that the Lord had SHOWN GREAT MERCY on her, and they rejoiced with her."   *(Amplified Version)*

The angel's words as recorded in Luke 1:20 also suggest

that God in His Sovereign love and kindness was going to perform the miracle in His appointed time, in spite of Zechariah's not believing God's promise.

In many books, we see quoted the example of Abraham trusting God to miraculously give him a son in seemingly impossible circumstances. I myself have used this example of Abraham in Chapter 19, "What Is The Biblical Type of Faith?", to establish a number of points.

But in order to have a **sound Biblical balance** in our understanding of God's teachings, we need to study not only the example of Abraham and similar examples which emphasise the importance in some situations of faith being expressed for God to perform a miracle. We need also to study other examples in God's Word, which show God performing miracles out of His sovereign mercy alone—without anyone trusting Him to perform the miracle.

WHERE IS YOUR FAITH?

Another clear example in the Holy Scriptures of God **sovereignly** in **His great mercy** and **love** performing a miracle to help some people, even though at the time they were exercising no faith in Him at all, is recorded in Luke 8:22-24:

"One day Jesus got into a boat with his disciples and said to them, 'Let us go across to the other side of the lake'. So they started out. As they were sailing, Jesus fell asleep. Suddenly a strong wind blew down on the lake, and the boat began to fill with water, so that they were all in great danger. The disciples went to Jesus and woke him up, saying, 'Master, Master! We are about to die!' Jesus got up and gave an order to the wind and to the stormy water; they quieted down, and there was a great calm." (Good News Version)

In this instance, the Lord Jesus had spoken to them in a way which **revealed God the Father's will.** Remember, the Lord Jesus never did or said anything which was not the Father's will (see John 5:19). This Word of the Lord was:

"Let us go across to the other side of the lake."
(Good News Version)

These words showed the disciples that God wanted to get them to the other side of the lake. This Word from the Lord Jesus gave them the God-given right to be sure that

151

His power would get them to the other side of the lake.

After sailing awhile, a strong wind caused their boat to begin to fill with water. The natural human minds of the disciples ignored what Jesus had said was the Father's will and were filled with fear. Even though they had a **promise** from God the Father, through the mouth of the Lord Jesus Christ, that they would get to the other side of the lake, they **did not believe** Him. Jesus' words to them in Luke 8:25 reveals their lack of faith in Him and His promise to them. Jesus said to the disciples:

> *"Where is your faith?"*   (Good News Version)

But the Lord Jesus in His Sovereign mercy and love still performed a miracle to help them. He did this **despite their lack of faith.** They did not exercise faith in their words or actions, but this did not stop Him from miraculously helping them by commanding the wind and the stormy water to be still.

PETER WALKING ON WATER

In Matthew 14:22-33, we see recorded a third example of God miraculously helping someone even though he was not believing Him to do so.

In this situation, the disciples were in a boat on the lake. Between three and six o'clock in the morning, the Lord Jesus began to walk on the water of the lake towards the boat. At first when they saw Him, the disciples were terrified, thinking He was a ghost. After they recognised that it was Jesus, He said, "Come", to the Apostle Peter. This Word revealed that it was the Father's will for Peter to be given His miraculous power to be able to walk on water from the boat to where the Lord Jesus was. At first, Peter trusted the Lord to give him power to do this. But note Matthew 14:30-31:

> *"But when he noticed the strong wind, he was AFRAID and started to sink down in the water. 'Save me, Lord!' he cried. At once Jesus reached out and grabbed hold of him and said, 'What LITTLE FAITH YOU HAVE. WHY DID YOU DOUBT?'"*
>
> (Good News Version)

These verses reveal that:
- because it was God the Father's will for Peter to walk on water—the Lord Jesus never did or said

anything that was not the Father's will (see John
5:19, 8:28, 12:49, and 14:10)—and because at
first, Peter trusted the Lord to give him power to
do so, miraculously the Lord helped him to do
this.

- because Peter began to doubt that the Lord would
  continue to enable him to walk on the water,
  the Lord ceased to allow His power to keep
  Peter walking on the water.

- as soon as Peter cried out to the Lord for help,
  the Lord saved him from drowning. Peter was
  full of doubts in the Lord when he asked the
  Lord for help, but miraculously the Lord **still
  saved him.**

Even though Peter changed from believing the Lord to
enable him to walk on water, to not trusting Him, the Lord
did not say to Peter, "You are not trusting Me to help you.
Since you are not exercising faith, I am not going to help
you. I am going to let you drown". The Lord answered
Peter's cry for help because of His **enormous love** and **sym-
pathy.**

Miraculously, the Lord will often help us just like this,
even when we are not exercising strong faith for Him to do
so. In His **tremendous mercy,** the Lord sometimes helps us
in spite of our feeble attempts to trust Him to do so.

In this example, the Lord answered Peter's request to
help him. This **does not mean that God helps us only when
we or someone else asks Him to help us.** There are probably
many times that we are **unaware** of in our lives that miraculously He has helped us or saved us from tragedy—keeping
a poisonous spider away from us and so on.

Many times, the Lord waits for us to ask Him to help
us, **so that we will recognise that He is the One Who is helping us.** Otherwise, we may think foolishly that help we
obtain when we are in desperate need is just luck or good
fortune or fate—which are evil pagan ideas.

There are some situations in which He will not help us
miraculously unless we ask and trust Him to do so. These
are the situations that He uses to teach us to trust in and
depend on Him more. These are **important learning times**
for us. For instance, in this example of Peter, the Lord in
mercy saved Peter miraculously from drowning despite his

lack of faith. But the Lord did not allow Peter to continue to walk on water when he began to doubt the Lord. This was to teach Peter the importance of trusting totally in the Lord.

FOOTNOTES:
1. Refer to Chapter 20, "False Understanding of What the Flesh and the World Are", in my book, "KEYS TO KNOWING GOD BETTER", for a detailed explanation of what the New Testament means by the expression "the world" and the difference between it and God's physical Earth.

2. Strong, op. cit., P.1189.

3. On salvation, the Book of Romans, Galatians and other parts of the Scriptures teach that unless a human agrees to respond with God-inspired faith to the movement of the Holy Spirit on his heart, leading him to repent of his sins and accept Jesus Christ as his Lord and Saviour, he will not become a born-again Christian and will not be saved.

22
When We Don't Know His Will

If the Scriptures do not reveal whether it is God the Father's will to ask for a particular miracle and His Holy Spirit has not given us specific guidance, we should not just add the words "If it be Thy will" to our request for such a miracle.

Instead, we should pray something along these lines: "Lord, I commit this situation totally into Your hands. I do not know what You want me to ask You to do. At this stage, I do not know if You want me even to ask You to do anything. I leave this whole situation completely in Your control."

The difference between "if it be Thy will" and the above, is that with the former, **we specify** certain alternatives that God can do, and if He doesn't answer this request relatively soon, we often **assume too readily** that it is not His will. For example, I once prayed, "Lord, if it be Your will for me to marry Rita (who later became my wife), lead her to come to talk to me and take a lot of interest in me after our church meetings." When God did not lead her to do the above within a number of months, I **superstitiously assumed** that it was not His will for me to marry her.

I was virtually commanding God how He had to reveal to me whether it was His will for me to marry her. This is another thing that is wrong about "if it be Thy will" prayers. They try to make God arrange our circumstances and sometimes those of other people, **in ways that we feel would show us His will.** We **have no right to try to order the Sovereign Lord of the Universe** specifically how He is to reveal His will to us. It is up to God to decide how He will reveal His will

155

to us—whether by the inner witness or inner voice of the Holy Spirit or by signs in our circumstances, or by dreams and other rarer, more spectacular means. The Bible mentions God revealing His will by these many different means. But the Bible does not promise us which of these specific means God will use to reveal His will to us—other than promising He will reveal His will by the Bible itself and by His Holy Spirit's guidance in general.

In the Scriptures, we see a number of examples of God revealing His will by signs in circumstances (see Jeremiah 32:6-8, 1 Samuel 10:1-9, Isaiah 7:10-14, 20:1-6, 37:30-32 and 38:1-8). Therefore, if God wishes to reveal His will to us by a sign in our circumstances, this is good. But just as we have no Biblical right to expect Him to give us a dream to guide us if He wants to speak to us by some other means, so too we have no Biblical right to expect Him to speak to us by signs in our circumstances. We are **not God's boss.**

It would have been far better if I had **not specified** to God any alternatives that He could do and instead said, "Lord, I commit this circumstance completely to Your control. I don't know whether You want me to marry this girl, so I'm not going to ask You to do anything specific, other than guide me by Your Spirit in the weeks, months or years ahead about whether You want me to marry her".

A **general** committing of this situation over to God when I did not know His will would have been far more sensible than praying as I did. In this way, I would have been leaving Him in charge to reveal His will in the way that **He felt was best,** not in the way I felt was best.

My future wife prayed a similar "if it be Thy will" prayer about me being able to see her and talk to her on a **specific day.** She said to the Lord that if He brought this situation about, she would take this as a **sign** that He wanted her to marry me. When God did not bring this circumstance about, **superstitiously,** she took this as a **sign** that God did not want her to marry me. Such wrong praying resulted later in her resisting the voice of the Holy Spirit for a few months when He spoke by putting thoughts in her mind that it was the Father's will for us to marry.

DON'T BE OVER-RELIANT ON SIGNS
Merely adding the words "if it be Thy will" to our

requests for specific miracles, instead of first seeking to find the Father's will from the Scriptures and His Holy Spirit's guidance, makes us **too reliant** on **"signs"** and **circumstances** in determining what His will is. We **wrongly begin to look to signs in our circumstances** as being **more important** in knowing God's will than the Scriptures and the Holy Spirit's guidance.

As shown in my book, "HOW TO RECOGNIZE GOD'S VOICE", **many times** our circumstances **do not reveal God's will** at all. For instance, if David had looked to his circumstances as his only or main indicator of God's will when Saul's soldiers were hunting for him, he would never have believed the Word of the Lord, spoken by the Holy Spirit to him, that he was going to be king (see 1 Chronicles 11:2).

My other book reveals also in great detail that even if we think God is revealing His will by signs in our circumstances, we must **check** to see if the Scriptures and the guidance of the Holy Spirit **confirm** to us what we think the seeming "sign" in our circumstances means. If you pray, "Lord, if it be Thy will, give me a job as a truck driver," and a few days later, an employer offers you a job as a truck driver, this does not mean necessarily this is God's will for you. You need to have the Holy Spirit really confirm to you that this job offer is a sign of the Father's will.

A number of years ago, I was seeking God's will as to whether to take a teaching job at a Christian school at a nearby city. When the head of the school offered me the job, if I had been superstitiously over-reliant on signs in my circumstances, I **would have got out of God's will.** When I continued to wait on God in prayer about this job for many hours, the Holy Spirit revealed to me that this job was not His will for me. He revealed that this seeming "sign" was not given by Him. This seeming "sign" was merely a result of the human reasoning of the head of the school.

In Isaiah 20:1-6, without inner guidance from the Holy Spirit, it would be impossible to relate circumstances of a prophet running around naked as being a sign of what was going to happen to Egypt and Sudan. A prophet running around naked could be taken as a sign that he was mad or a sign of thousands of other things, if God's Spirit had not given a revelation of what this circumstance meant.

Circumstances **alone** are not a reliable indicator of God's will.

157

Refer to Chapter 8 of "HOW TO RECOGNIZE GOD'S VOICE" for more details on signs and circumstances.

Many people throughout history have wrongly prayed, "Lord, if it be Your will do so and so....If it is not Your will, don't do it." Then they have wrongly determined what God's will was by what **happened in circumstances just after then.** Many times, God's will was what they asked Him to do originally, but because He did not do it in the short time after they asked, they wrongly assumed that it was not His will. They should have waited for the guidance of the Holy Spirit, instead of being over-reliant on looking for signs in their short-term circumstances.

God wanted to answer their prayer requests. But He wanted to answer them a long while into the future.

As well as committing ourselves over to God in the way suggested above, we must also be ready in case in following days or months, the Holy Spirit reveals specifically what the Father wants us to ask Him to do.

OLD TESTAMENT EXCEPTIONS

In the Old Testament, there are two examples of believers asking God to reveal His will to them by specific signs in their circumstances. These are recorded in Genesis 24:10-27 and Judges 6:36-40. In both instances, God answered their requests by giving them the specific signs they requested.

But note there is **no promise** given in the Scriptures that God will give us the specific sign we may request. Therefore, we cannot use the above two examples to suggest that He will give us the specific sign we may request.

We must remember that in Old Testament times, only a very small number of believers were given the Holy Spirit. These were prophets and some of the leaders of Israel. Even these people did not have the Holy Spirit in the same measure that a born-again believer would in New Testament times (see John 7:39, Ezekiel 36:22-29). As a result, in Old Testament times, God used sometimes some **external** forms of guidance He no longer uses. On occasion, God used Urim and Thummin—we are not sure what these were, but they were worn on the breast of the High Priest's clothes (see Exodus 28:15-30)—to guide the people of Israel. In the New Testament, there is no mention of God using the Urim and Thummin anymore to guide His people. The New

Testament makes it clear that after the death and resurrection of the Lord Jesus, the Father desires to guide His people primarily by His Scriptures (see 2 Timothy 3:16, 2 Peter 1:20-21), secondly by the guidance of His Holy Spirit (see John 16:13, 10:27), thirdly by whatever sign in our circumstances He chooses to give and fourthly but more rarely by dreams or other more spectacular forms of guidance. (Refer to my book "HOW TO RECOGNIZE GOD'S VOICE" for more details.)

In great kindness and mercy, God gave Abraham's servant the sign in his circumstances he requested. There is no mention in the Bible of Abraham's servant having the Holy Spirit. The Urim and Thummin were not in existence then. Therefore, as an **exception,** God revealed His will by giving Abraham's servant the sign he requested.

In the second example, recorded in Judges 6:36-40, we see that God gave Gideon the two signs he requested. But note God did this as an exception also. Only minutes, hours, days or weeks before, Gideon had received the Holy Spirit (see Judges 6:34). So previously, he had precious little time to learn how to recognize the voice of the Holy Spirit in his thoughts. God would have taken this into consideration.

Note also that God had already revealed His will previously to Gideon about the same matter (see Judges 6:11-16). God revealed His will through the words of His angel and through His angel giving Gideon a specific sign that He wished to give. Some may argue that Gideon was tempting God greatly by asking for two further signs after all this.

But in great compassion and kindness again, God gave Gideon the two specific signs he requested.

It is little wonder that as an exception, God did this for Gideon. Later in Judges 8:22-27, we see how confused Gideon was in determining God's will. First, when asked to be the ruler of Israel, he said rightly that the Lord should be their ruler, not him or his sons. Then immediately after, he made an idol of gold. This was a terrible sin. He seemed to have no understanding that previously, God had commanded all Israelites to never make idols (see Exodus 20:4-5).

(For more details why it is wrong for us to pray "if it be Thy will" and why it is impossible for us to pray an equivalent of Jesus' prayer in Luke 22:42, refer to my booklet "MIRACLES—AND IF IT BE THY WILL".)

23
Miracles Requiring Holy Spirit Revelation

(N.B. This and the next five chapters were written in late 1982 and early 1983).

Many ask, "What are examples of miracles that the Scriptures do not specifically promise?" Here are a few. These are mainly spectacular examples. There are obviously many less spectacular examples that could be included here.

Suppose an occultist or wicked person was doing things to try to prevent Christianity spreading. In this situation, we could trust God to cause him to go blind for a time only if the Lord Jesus by the inner guidance of the Holy Spirit told us that He wanted us to expect such a miracle.

As recorded in Acts 13:6-12, Paul trusted the Lord to perform such a miracle. He trusted God to make the occult-witchcraft leader Elymas blind for a short period. The Lord never gave any specific promise in the Bible saying that we could pray in certainty for someone to go blind. But in Paul's case, verse 9 says that he was **filled** and **controlled** by **God the Holy Spirit** when he was trusting God to perform this miracle. As Romans 8:26-27 infers, when our request to God is based on the inner guidance of His Holy Spirit, He will certainly answer. Romans 8:26 says that the Holy Spirit will help us pray according to God's will, and 1 John 5:14-15 says that if we ask according to God's will, He will **surely** give us exactly what we ask.

When Paul trusted God the Father to make this wicked occultist go blind, we know that His Holy Spirit must have told him that it was the Father's will for him to believe for this miracle. Verses 9 to 11 say that Paul was filled and controlled by the Holy Spirit at **exactly the same time** as he was in certainty trusting God for this miracle. The Scriptures would not say that Paul was filled and controlled by the Holy Spirit at that point, if his thinking was and actions were in disagreement with the Father's will.

It is impossible to pray contrary to God's will, if our thoughts are controlled by God the Holy Spirit at that point of time.

A second example of a miracle that requires Holy Spirit revelation is if we are heading out to sea in a rip and would drown because no other person is on the beach and we are not a strong enough swimmer to get back onto the shore. In this situation, we can believe that God is going to pick us up and carry us in the air back to shore, if God the Holy Spirit speaks to us that He wants us to trust Him for this miracle. If we are uncertain that God will do this, even after His Spirit has revealed His will to us, this lack of expressing God-inspired faith will prevent the miracle, if this is a situation in which God requires us to trust Him to do the miracle before He will do it.

In another instance, if we are about to be attacked by a savage dog or a snake, and the Holy Spirit reveals to us that it is the Father's will to paralyse the dog or snake until we get away, then we have the God-given right to believe with absolute certainty that He will perform this miracle for us.

If God does not specifically reveal His will in the above two situations, we should pray something like, "Lord, here am I. I need Your help whatever it is." Then we should trust that He will work the situation out in the ways that He knows are best.

If we are in a drought and have no food left, we can believe that God the Father will send birds to feed us, if the Holy Spirit reveals to us that it is His will to feed us this way.

If God doesn't specifically reveal to us that this is His will, we can trust Him to feed us, by any means at all, on the basis of such Scriptures as Acts 14:17 and Psalms 136:25. However, we cannot **specifically** in certainty trust that God will feed us by birds unless He tells us that this is the way that He wants to feed us. This is proven in the Bible: the only Bible character who ever trusted God to be fed by birds in a time of drought was Elijah.

Note, though, that Elijah had guidance from God to tell him that it was God's will for him to trust God for this miracle, as 1 Kings 17:2-4 says:

> *"Then the Lord said to Elijah, 'Leave this place and go east and hide yourself near Cherith Brook, east of the Jordan. The brook will supply you with water to drink, and I have commanded ravens to bring you food there'."* *(Good News Version)*

Elijah didn't trust God for this miracle on the basis of a promise from the Bible, but a Word from the Holy Spirit. If we tried to pray for God to feed us by birds, we could not expect with certainty that this miracle would happen unless He spoke a Word to us beforehand. Without this Word from God, we would not know His will. As a result, 1 John 5:14-15 suggests that we couldn't be sure that He would answer.

OTHER EXAMPLES

We could only trust God the Father for all of the following miracles to occur if the Holy Spirit revealed to us **beforehand** that it was the Father's will. The Bible doesn't specifically promise us these types of miracles:

- Revelation 11:6 shows that if God the Holy Spirit spoke to us saying that it was the Father's will for us to with certainty trust Him to make it no longer rain, to make rivers and lakes be turned into blood and to stop preventing Satan from putting sickness on people (see Job 2:4-7), we would have a God-given right to expect these miracles.

  We could only do this if God gave us inner guidance to do so, because verse 6 says that two men could trust God to do these things only because "they have authority" (from God). God would only lead someone to trust Him to cause a famine to occur, if it would lead thousands of unbelievers to Himself, or achieve another great purpose.

- The next example is God stopping the sun and moon in the sky. In faith, Joshua commanded the sun and the moon to be still. In response, the Lord performed this miracle because it was His will. (see Joshua 10:12-14). We could only trust God for this if He told us it was His will.

- A further example is the miracle of being given superhuman strength which enables even a normal man or woman to be physically stronger than all other people.

  Samson was an example of this. God gave Samson guidance that it was His will for Samson to have this strength. Some people (including some religious leaders) talk about Samson as though he was only a fairy story. They say that his strength was in his hair. This idea is foolishness. The only reason God stopped giving Samson His supernatural strength was that Samson **disobeyed the Word of the Lord** spoken by God to him (see Judges 13:3-5). In this Word, God commanded him to never allow his hair to be cut. Judges 16:4-20 records that he allowed his hair to be cut.

  In the movies, Samson always has big muscles. However, in reality he may have only been a weak, skinny, bony fellow who became incredibly strong only when the Holy Spirit came on him to give him this supernatural strength. Instances of the Holy Spirit giving him extraordinary strength are in Judges 13:25, 14:6, and 15:14. Samson was no fairy story.

- Another example is the miracle of having the Holy Spirit open or knock down a door of a prison in which some anti-Christian Government has put us (see Acts 5:19 and 12:7-10).

- Yet another example is the miracle of being able to run faster than horses. This miracle happened to Elijah. He ran almost 20 miles to the city of Jezreel, faster than King Ahab's horses. Even though the Scriptures never promise this miracle to all who desire it, Elijah was sensitive enough to the guidance of the Holy Spirit to know that it was His will for him to be absolutely sure that this miracle would occur. Elijah didn't doubt that the miracle would occur. Otherwise, the miracle possibly would never have occurred (see 1 Kings 18:45-46).

- We shouldn't try to trust God to raise from the dead every person who dies this year. We should only attempt to exercise faith for those individuals who have died whom the Holy Spirit tells us to do this

163

for (see Romans 8:26). If God the Father answered every request that we could pray about raising people from the dead, this would prevent humans from ever dying and then going to heaven or hell. Such a situation would be clearly contrary to His will as revealed in His Scriptures. Many people forget that even though the Lord Jesus raised Lazarus from the dead, Lazarus still died years later. God did not raise him a second time.

If we try to trust God the Father that a person, whom His Holy Spirit hasn't told us that it is the Father's will he be raised from the dead, we will fail. This is because we won't have any Word of the Lord from the Holy Spirit which will give us the faith to believe for this miracle. (see Romans 10:17).

- In times of famine, we cannot trust God to miraculously make our jar of flour and our tin of fruit to continue being full each day, after we have used some of it for our meals each day, unless He gives us guidance that it is His will that we trust Him for this. In 1 Kings 17:10-16, we see that Elijah trusted God for such a miracle.

- We can also only trust God to miraculously carry us from one continent to another (for example, in times when weather conditions make aircraft travel impossible) if minutes, hours or days before this, He has revealed to us that He wants us to trust Him to perform this miracle. In the Book of Acts, it records that the evangelist Philip was taken by the Holy Spirit from one place to another in a second (see Acts 8:39-40).

PAUL IN DANGER OF DROWNING

When Paul was being taken as a prisoner to ancient Italy, as they neared the coast of the Island of Crete in the Mediterranean Sea, God allowed a strong wind known as "The North Easter" to blow the ship off course, towards the coast of Libya in North Africa. (Check a map to help picture the scene.) Their ship was battered by a violent storm. However, even though Paul could have attempted to believe that the ship miraculously would not sink, he did not (see Acts 27:1-44).

Paul knew that the Lord Jesus easily calmed a similar

terrible storm on Lake Galilee (see Mark 4:35-41). So why didn't Paul try to trust that the Father would calm this storm also?

Paul also knew that Peter had walked on water in the historical event recorded in Matthew 14:22-31, but Paul didn't try to trust God to miraculously enable him to escape death by walking on the water to the safety of Libya or the islands of Crete or Cyprus or somewhere else. Why didn't Paul attempt to trust God the Holy Spirit to carry him miles through the air just as He did for Philip the evangelist? In Acts 8:39-40, we see that after Philip revealed the meaning of the Scriptures to the palace official from Ethiopia, the Holy Spirit took him through the air in a second of time from just near Jerusalem to the city of Ashdod. This is a distance of about 33 miles. Imagine a town 33 miles away from us. That is how far the Spirit of the Lord carried him.[1] But Paul didn't attempt to trust God for this miracle to save his life either.

Why not? This is because he knew that no Christian can ever trust God to cause these sorts of miracles to happen, unless, before trying to believe with certainty that the miracle is going to occur, the Holy Spirit reveals (through the inner witness, inner voice, dreams and so on) that it is God the Father's will for this miracle to occur.

Paul didn't try to believe with absolute assurance for the sort of miracle that he may have preferred. Instead, Paul would only trust God the Father to perform what He had shown, through the words of an angel, was His will. Acts 27:22-25 reveals this when Paul, talking to the men on the ship, said:

> *"But now I beg you, take courage! Not one of you will lose his life; only the ship will be lost. For last night an angel of the God to whom I belong and whom I worship came to me and said, 'Don't be afraid, Paul! You must stand before the Emperor. And God in His goodness to you has spared the lives of all those who are sailing with you.' So take courage, men! For I TRUST in God that it will be JUST AS I WAS TOLD."*   *(Good News Version)*

Note these last words of Paul. He was only trusting God for the miracle that he was told to trust God for. He didn't try to trust God for something that he was not told by God.

After having this Word of guidance from God, note that Paul didn't pray "If it be Thy will", or "I **hope** you will perform this miracle, Lord." No, instead he trusted God to cause this miracle to happen. His certain attitude is seen in his words to the men on the ship. He said in verse 25, *"So take courage men! For I trust in God that it **will** be just as I was **told**."*

He didn't allow his mind to have any doubt about the miracle occurring. He didn't say, "For I trust in God that **possibly,** or **maybe,** this miracle will take place." Paul's certainty is expressed in the Amplified Version, which says:

> *"So keep up your courage, men, for I have faith— COMPLETE CONFIDENCE—in God that it will be EXACTLY as it was told me."*

FOOTNOTE:

1. It is possible that the Holy Spirit in **His Sovereignty** may have taken Philip through the air without first revealing to Philip that this was His will and without Philip being certain this miracle was going to happen. But it is just as possible that the Holy Spirit did reveal to Philip that it was the Father's will and that Philip had to exercise certain faith that this would occur. The Scriptures do not reveal which of these alternatives is true.

24
Moses—A Great Example

Moses knew how to trust God to perform miracles. If we study the following Scriptures, we will see that Moses only believed for a miracle **after** God had spoken to him, assuring him that the miracle was God's will.

A STICK TURNS INTO A SNAKE

Moses and Aaron only trusted the Lord to perform the miracle of the walking stick turning into a snake **after** the Lord as recorded in Exodus 7:8-9, had revealed to them that this miracle was His will. They didn't decide themselves to try to believe for this miracle. Obedience to God's guidance is a key element in trusting Him to perform miracles. Exodus 7:10 infers this:

> *"So Moses and Aaron went to the king and DID AS THE LORD HAD COMMANDED."*
> *(Good News Version)*

Obedience to God's guidance also occurred in Exodus 7:14-18, when God led Moses to trust Him that when Moses struck the surface of the Nile River in Egypt with a stick, He would cause a miracle to occur. God said that this miracle would make the water of the Nile River turn into blood, killing all the fish in it, and making the water undrinkable for the Egyptians.

Exodus 7:19 records that God spoke a revelation to Moses guiding him and Aaron to trust God for another miracle. This second miracle involved the turning into blood of all other sources and containers of water in Egypt— the rivers, canals, pools and even the wooden tubs and stone jars. Exodus 7:20 reveals again the obedience of Moses and

Aaron to these Words of the Lord spoken in relation to trusting God for the miracle:

"Then Moses and Aaron DID AS THE LORD COMMANDED."   *(Good News Version)*

PRINCIPLES OF TRUSTING GOD FOR MIRACLES NOT SPECIFICALLY PROMISED IN SCRIPTURE

The principles involved in trusting God for such miracles are: first, having the Holy Spirit reveal to us **what** and **how** to pray; and then doing as God commands by trusting Him not for what miracle we want, but for the miracle that He wants.

For example, if God tells us to blow a trumpet, or hit a rock, or just sit there, trusting Him for the miracle, then we must **obey** Him. If God tells us to walk around the city walls for seven days believing He will cause the walls of Jericho to fall down on the seventh day (as He commanded Joshua to), we must not walk around the walls for five days expecting the walls to fall down. We must **obey** the Holy Spirit's instructions **to the finest detail** when trusting Him to perform a miracle.

The third principle of trusting God for miracles not specifically promised in the Scriptures, is that we must express in our **thoughts, words** and **actions** that we are certain that the miracle will occur. This is followed by the miracle then occurring at that time or in the future.

The following examples will show that the above three principles are things that in many instances, God wishes us to follow.

GOD GUIDED MOSES TO TRUST HIM FOR A FROG PLAGUE

The next miracle that God led Moses to trust Him for was a plague of frogs. God led Moses to first get Aaron to hold out his walking stick over the rivers, canals and pools of Egypt. God also led Moses and Aaron to believe in certainty that a plague of frogs would occur while Aaron did this. Moses and Aaron trusted that God would force these frogs to come out of the rivers and water places and spread all over Egypt. This is recorded in Exodus 8:1-5.

Exodus 8:6 shows that Aaron obeyed in faith the Word

of the Lord spoken to him by God. **Then** the miracle occurred.

Moses and Aaron are nowhere to be seen saying, "If it be Thy will Lord, let frogs come over the land of Egypt." Nor did Moses and Aaron pray faithless "hope" prayers such as, "Lord, I hope that You will send frogs over the land of Egypt." Nor do we see in the record of the Bible, Moses going to Pharoah and saying, "God is going to send a frog plague on Egypt today, **if it be His will.**" Some church-goers, if they were Moses, would have done these things.

GOD'S NEXT MIRACLE

Observe another miracle that Moses trusted God to perform. This is recorded in Exodus 8:20-24. In these verses, it says that God desired to send a swarm of flies which would make life very hard for the Egyptians, but would not affect the Hebrews. Moses trusted God for this miracle to occur, and it did.

Even though the Bible doesn't specifically mention Moses exercising God-inspired faith here in this example, it is easily assumed that he did. This is because when God told the people of Israel to cross the Red Sea, He promised to, by a miracle, separate the deep waters. But no mention in Exodus Chapter 14 is made of the inference that for the miracle to occur, the Lord required the Israelites to exercise faith. However, Hebrews 11:29 infers that at least some of the Israelites had exercised God-inspired faith that a miracle would occur that day, and that this is the reason God performed the miracle:

"It was FAITH that made the Israelites able to cross the Red Sea as if on dry land." (Good News Version)

The same applies to the miracle of the Passover. This miracle is recorded in Exodus Chapter 12. In these verses, no mention is made of God-inspired faith being required by God before He would perform the Passover miracle. However, Hebrews 11:28 establishes the importance of the **faith** of Moses in the Word of the Lord that God spoke to him in this situation.

A third example in the Bible of a miracle occurring without God-inspired faith being said in surrounding verses to be the cause of it occurring, but this being mentioned in another part of the Bible, was the miracle of the walls of

Jericho falling down. This miracle is seen in Joshua 6:1-21. In these verses, no mention of the fact that God performed the miracle as a result of faith in a Word of the Lord is made. But later in Hebrews 11:30, God reveals:

"It was FAITH that made the walls of Jericho fall down after the Israelites had marched around them for seven days."   *(Good News Version)*

This proves that just because the Scripture relating a miracle occurring doesn't mention faith being exercised, this doesn't mean that God-inspired faith wasn't required by God before He would perform the miracle.

Note that this abovementioned miracle of the flies shows that we can only be assured that the miracle is going to occur on a particular day if God reveals to us that the miracle is going to occur on that day.

Exodus 8:23 says that God told Moses that the miracle would take place on the next day. Once God had said this, Moses could be assured about when the miracle would take place. If God doesn't reveal when the physical manifestation of the miracle will occur, one must stand in faith believing that God will **certainly** (**not maybe**) cause the miracle to happen sometime in the future.

Too many people **try to tell God when** to perform a miracle, when He has not revealed to them when He wants to perform it.

IMPORTANCE OF OBEYING GOD'S SPIRIT'S GUIDANCE

Moses' trust in God, his keenness to find out God's will and his obedience to the Words spoken by God are seen in Exodus 9:22-26. God told Moses in Exodus 9:22 to raise his hand toward the sky when trusting Him to perform the miracle of causing hail to fall on the people, plants and animals in Egypt. Moses didn't strike the ground with his stick (which God had told Aaron to do when trusting God to perform the miracle of dust turning into gnats—Exodus 8:17). Nor did he hold his walking stick out over the rivers, canals and pools (which God had told Moses to get Aaron to do when trusting God to perform the miracle of the plague of frogs—Exodus 8:5). Nor did he take a few handfuls of ash from a furnace and throw them into the air in front of the king (which God had told Moses to do when he was to trust

God to allow boils to come on the Egyptians and their animals— Exodus 9:8). Nor did Moses believe God for this miracle by pointing at the trees, or by kicking the ground or by running around a building.

In Exodus 9:23, Moses is seen **obeying exactly** the instructions that God told him to do when he was to trust God for the hail. Faith and obedience are **two sides** of **the same coin.** James 2:26 shows that actions of obedience express our faith.

There is nothing magical about raising our hand towards the sky. We could do this all night long and no miracle would happen. But when we, or Moses, are given an instruction by God to do a particular thing (no matter how silly it may seem) while trusting Him to perform a miracle, then our **obedience,** or that of Moses, and God-inspired **faith in** this Word of the Lord, will be what God requires us to do or express for Him to perform the miracle. God uses such occasions to **train us to trust Him.**

God told Moses and Aaron to do **different** things for each miracle for which they trusted Him. They were told on one occasion to throw ash and on another occasion to wave a walking stick over the rivers and canals. God did not tell them to do these things as though they were some magical formula which always results in Him performing a miracle.

God **didn't need** to have Aaron and Moses throw ash, or wave a walking stick or raise their hands to the sky, as a cause of the miracles occurring. God has infinite power and therefore **does not need our puny human efforts to help Him.** But God used these simple, seemingly useless commands to test and strengthen Moses and Aaron's trust in and obedience to Him, just as He may do with us.

The importance of obedience to God's inner guidance in trusting Him for the type of miracles not specifically promised in the Scriptures is **tragically overlooked** by many Christians.

The Lord Jesus didn't always perform miracles with the same outward manifestations. At one time, He put spittle in a blind person's eyes and at another time, He did something different—telling the blind person, without putting spit in the eyes, that he was healed (see Mark 8:22-26 and Mark 10:46-52).

OTHER SIGNS AND WONDERS AND
MOSES' CERTAINTY

In the miracles of God creating a plague of gnats out of dust (see Exodus 8:16-19); the animals owned by the Egyptians dying (see Exodus 9:1-6); God sending the worst hailstorm on Egypt in its history (see Exodus 9:13-26); God sending a plague of locusts upon Egypt (see Exodus 10:1-15); total darkness occurring in the daytime (see Exodus 10:21-23); death visiting the first-born son of every Egyptian family but not the Israelite families (see Exodus 11:1-12:36); the opening of the waters of the Red Sea (see Exodus Chapter 14); bitter water becoming pure (see Exodus 15:22-25); manna and quails appearing from nowhere on the days that Moses predicted, and the many other miracles recorded in the Book of Numbers, we see the same Biblical principles operating. First, God gave a Word of the Lord to the mind of Moses which showed Moses what specific miracles God wanted Moses to trust Him to perform. Then Moses in **absolute certainty** trusted Him that these miracles that God specifically promised would happen. Nowhere in these examples do we see Moses or Aaron praying "if it be Thy will" or "I hope God will answer" about these miracles.

25
Joshua

Joshua knew also how to trust God for miracles. In Joshua 3:7-17, Joshua is seen to trust God to stop the Jordan River from flowing so that the people of Israel could cross over on dry earth. The nation of Israel had been wandering in the desert for 40 years and was now ready to possess the Promised Land of Canaan.

Note that Joshua didn't decide himself to try to believe God for this miracle. First, Joshua listened to God. God told Joshua that it was His will briefly to stop the Jordan River from flowing. This Word of the Lord is seen in Joshua 3:7-13. Whenever the Bible says, "The Lord said", this is a Word of the Lord to a person or a number of people.

Note also that Joshua didn't doubt that this Word of the Lord would come true. Instead, he was **certain** that the miracle would happen. This was a great test of faith for Joshua, because, as verse 14 says, the Jordan River was in flood at the time. To the natural human mind, it would have been easier to exercise faith if the Jordan River had a low level of water in it. But since the high, very fast-flowing waters of the Jordan River were clearly visible to the eyes of Joshua, his natural human tendency would have been to doubt this Word of the Lord.

However, Joshua chose to ignore the bad circumstances his eyes saw—a flooded dangerous river. Because what he was trusting God to do was God's will, he was certain it would come to pass.

Joshua didn't pray "If it be Thy will" prayers in this matter. Check the Bible! Neither did he say, "Lord, I **hope** that this miracle will happen", or, "Lord, I believe that **possibly** this miracle will happen." We can see that Joshua didn't do these things because in Joshua 3:9-13, he is recorded as telling the people of Israel that the miracle would **surely** happen. Joshua said in verse 13:

"When the priests who carry the Covenant Box of the Lord of all the earth put their feet in the water, the Jordan WILL stop flowing, and the water coming downstream WILL pile up in one place."

(Good News Version)

Joshua and the priests, as well as believing God to perform the miracle, **obeyed exactly** the instructions that God gave them as recorded in Joshua 3:7-8. Joshua didn't try to copy the things that Moses did when trusting the Lord for miracles. Just because God told Moses to strike the surface of the Nile River with a stick while trusting Him for the miracle of the water turning into blood, this didn't encourage Joshua to strike the Jordan River while trusting God to make the river water stop flowing. There is nothing miracle-producing about striking the surface of a river with a stick, unless God the Holy Spirit tells us to do this in relation to a specific miracle He desires to perform.

As a result of the Israelites' trust in the Word of the Lord, and obedience to His minutest instructions, the Holy Spirit stopped the flow of the high, fast-flowing flood waters just long enough for the thousands of Israelites to cross over. The faith of Joshua is a good example for us (see Joshua 3:7-17).

THE HOLY SPIRIT KNOCKS A CITY'S WALLS OVER

The next example which shows how Joshua trusted God for miracles is seen at the city of Jericho. This is recorded in Joshua Chapter 6. Here, we see that the nation of Israel, after miraculously crossing the dangerous Jordan River, then camped outside the city of Jericho. Jericho had an army and many evil inhabitants. It was defended by a powerful wall surrounding it. The nation of Israel had no natural means of knocking the wall over, such as battering rams.

If we were Joshua, how would we face this military problem? Joshua knew the answer. He waited on God until God revealed what miracle He desired to perform.

God told Joshua that **if** he, seven priests and the army of Israel marched around the city of Jericho once a day for six days and then on the seventh day, marched around the city seven times while the priests blew their trumpets and the soldiers shouted as the seven priests played a long note on their trumpets, then He would miraculously cause the walls of Jericho to fall down. They obeyed and the walls fell down (see Joshua 6:2-21).

The miracle of Jericho's walls falling down did not occur because soldiers and priests walked around the walls a number of times shouting and playing trumpets at a particular time. A number of us today could walk around the walls of any city and no such miracle would happen, unless the Holy Spirit had given us a Word of the Lord telling us that He wanted us to do this.

This miracle of Jericho's walls falling down only happened for Joshua because:

- God spoke to Joshua telling him **what** to trust Him for in this circumstance.
- This Word of the Lord gave Joshua the God-imparted ability to exercise faith for this specific miracle.
- Joshua put this God-given faith into practice in his thoughts, words and actions. Hebrews 11:30 says:

"It was FAITH that made the walls of Jericho fall down after the Israelites had marched around them for seven days."   *(Good News Version)*

MIRACLES AT AI

Other miracles that God did in Joshua's life occurred in the same way. For example, in Joshua 8:1-2, it says that God gave him guidance about how to defeat the pagan, idol-worshipping people of Ai. Joshua's actions recorded in Joshua 8:3-29, and his words recorded in Joshua 8:7-8, show that he didn't doubt for one minute that this miracle would occur. As a result, the miracle did occur.

Joshua exercised faith for these miracles in the way that God told him, and not as his commonsense or human reasoning would have decided.

There is much to learn from Joshua's life as recorded in the Holy Scriptures.

26
Daniel

The prophet Daniel was another who knew how to trust God for miracles. He didn't pray in presumption, or "If it be Thy will", or "I hope God has answered" prayers in relation to miracles. He knew how to find God's will first and then pray in faith-filled **assurance** that whatever miracle God led him to trust Him for, would come to pass.

Even though this book is not about praying for miraculous events promised specifically in Scripture, Daniel will be used as one example of this.

In Daniel 9:2, we see Daniel found God's will about a specific matter by studying the Scriptures. Daniel found in Jeremiah 25:11-12 and 29:10 that God had told Jeremiah that Jerusalem would remain desolate for 70 years after King Nebuchadnezzar of Babylon took the Jews into captivity in Babylon. Jeremiah 29:10 also revealed that it was God's will for some of these Jews taken captive to Babylon, to return to Jerusalem and Judea to rebuild Jerusalem and their nation.

Daniel 9:3-19 reveals that then Daniel prayed in certainty for these things to be brought about by God.

God answered Daniel's prayer request on the same day that Daniel trusted God to bring about His Word. Verse 2 shows where Daniel found out God's will about what he should pray. Verses 3-19 reveal Daniel's faith in this Word from God. Verses 16 and 17 show how Daniel asked God to do what He had promised Jeremiah that He would do. Daniel's faith for this miracle was based on God's will—His Word.

Verses 20-23 of Daniel 9 reveal a very important lesson. From the **same moment in time** that Daniel prayed in faith on the basis of God's Word, God said that Daniel's prayer request was granted. But the **manifestation in the physical world** of God's answer to this prayer of faith in His Word didn't occur **until later.** Daniel had to believe that God had already answered his prayer, even though he would be aware in the physical world that Jerusalem and God's Temple were still desolate.

What may have happened if Daniel began to doubt God's Word, when he didn't see the answer in the physical world straight away?

27
Elijah

Elijah was another man who knew how to find God's will and how to trust God for miracles. If we study 1 Kings 17 to 21, we will find that there are many examples of Elijah being able to recognize the guidance of the Holy Spirit and trusting God for those miracles that He had shown were His will (see 1 Kings 17:2, 8, 14; 18:1; 19:11, 13, 15-18; 21:17-19, 21-24, 28).

Elijah tried to exercise faith for miracles only when God assured him that it was His will for Elijah to trust Him for these miracles. There are a number of incidents which reveal this.

First, 1 Kings 17:13-16 tells how Elijah trusted God for the miracle of a handful of flour and a jar containing some olive oil to continue to feed him, the widow and her son during 3 1/2 years of famine. Elijah didn't just decide to try to believe God for this miracle, without first having Him reveal His will in the matter. Elijah didn't pray in presumption. Instead, as verse 14 shows, Elijah exercised faith for this miracle only **after** God had assured him that it was His will.

The second incident which suggests that Elijah only trusted God to perform miracles AFTER God told him what was His specific will is 1 Kings 18:36. In this verse, Elijah said that he only set up the altar in front of the people of Israel and the Baal prophets so that he could trust God for a miracle, because God told him to do so. Verse 36 ends with:

".....I am your servant and I HAVE DONE ALL THIS AT YOUR COMMAND."(Good News Version)

ELIJAH PRAYS FOR FAMINE
In 1 Kings 17 and 18, we see that Elijah prayed for an

Israelite nation whose sins were similar to those of many nations today, to have a famine.

The Israelites at the time of Elijah were all, except for 7,001 people, involved with the Baal religion. The Baal religion involved drunkenness, immorality, homosexuality, drug-taking, witchcraft-occult, violence in the form of child-sacrifice, temple prostitution with Baal priests and priest-esses and so on. God said in 1 Kings 19:18 that 7,000 Israe-lites had remained true to Him and had not backslidden. Elijah himself was the other person.

James 5:17-18 says:

> *"Elijah was a human being with a nature such as we have—with feelings, affections and constitution as our-selves; and he prayed earnestly for it not to rain, and no rain fell on the earth for three years and six months. And [then] he prayed again and the heavens supplied rain and the land produced its crops [as usual]."*
> *(Amplified Version)*

God did not answer Elijah's request as a so-called "reward" for Elijah's holy life or because Elijah was suppos-edly God's favourite. As James 5:17 says, Elijah had a sinful nature just like anyone else, and as stated previously, God answers prayer requests not on the basis of how good we are.

If we just read James 5:17-18, we can wrongly assume that God caused the rain to stop falling for 3 1/2 years and then caused it to begin falling at the end of this time, just because Elijah asked Him to do this. But when we take James 5:17-18 in relation to 1 Kings 18:1, we see that God led Elijah to pray for these miraculous events. Elijah did not just say to himself, "It is about time I prayed for a fam-ine" or 3 1/2 years later, "I now desire to pray for rain." 1 Kings 18:1 says:

> *"After many days, the WORD OF THE LORD came to Elijah in the third year, saying, 'Go, show yourself to Ahab, and I will send rain upon the earth'."*
> *(Amplified Version)*

Just after Elijah first trusted that God would stop it from raining, some other Israelites were probably praying in pre-sumption, asking God to cause it to rain. But the Lord **ignored** their prayer requests. This shows that the important

179

thing to God is **not how many people** ask Him for something, but whether we are praying what He is leading us to request.

If God answers presumption prayer requests, He would have had to answer Elijah who was praying for drought and answer the prayer requests of those Israelites praying for rain. In 99% of cases, God answers only prayer requests based on His will.

Nowhere in the Bible does it say that Elijah prayed, "If it be Thy will, Lord, send no rain for 3 1/2 years," or "Lord, I hope that you will prevent it from raining for 3 1/2 years." Instead, Elijah sought to know for what God wanted him to exercise faith.

PRAYER FOR FOOD AND WATER IN THE FAMINE

During the time of the 3 1/2 years' famine, God told Elijah to go to a particular brook where He had commanded ravens to feed him. 1 Kings 17:2-3 says:

> *"Then THE LORD SAID to Elijah, 'Leave this place and go east and hide yourself near Cherith Brook, east of the Jordan. The brook will supply you with water to drink, and I have commanded ravens to bring you food there'."* (Good News Version)

This was the Word of the Lord for Elijah at this time. It revealed God's will.

Elijah didn't go down to the Jordan River thinking that he would trust God for the miraculous provision of food and water there. Nor did he go down to Egypt where he could have obtained water from the Nile River and food from the land there. He could have falsely reasoned to himself that just because Jacob and his sons went down to Egypt to find water and food in the famine recorded in Genesis 42 and 43, he should do the same. Some churchgoers would say that if Elijah did this, he would be going down to Egypt "stepping out in faith" for God to feed him. If Elijah had gone to Egypt to look for food and water, this wouldn't have been Biblical trust at all; it would have been disobedience to the guidance of the Holy Spirit as recorded in 1 Kings 17:2-3. Trust in God is expressed in obedience.

I've known of some churchgoers with a strange concept of trusting God. They thought that trusting God **was doing**

what they thought was best, and **then asking God to bless their efforts.** This is wrongly attempting to make God **our servant.**

Elijah's obedience to God's guidance about the matter of **what** miracle to trust Him for and **how** to trust Him for it, is seen in 1 Kings 17:5:

> *"Elijah obeyed the Lord's command, and went and stayed by Cherith Brook."*   (Good News Version)

As a result of Elijah's obedience to the guidance of the Holy Spirit— acting on the Word of the Lord—and faith that this miracle would certainly come to pass, God performed the miracle. Verse 6 records that ravens were instructed by the Lord to bring him bread and meat from somewhere, each morning and evening.

Elijah's attitude of only attempting to trust God for the specific miracles that God had revealed were His will is also seen in 1 Kings 17:8-9. Here God told Elijah to go to the town of Zarephath in ancient Lebanon—in a time of no rain, very little food or no food at all in some areas—and to expect that a widow, whom to Elijah's natural mind would probably be thought to be starving, would feed him. Elijah **obeyed** God's guidance.

He didn't say to God, "Lord, since You have fed me by ravens at this Cherith Brook, I am now going to trust You to make water come bubbling up out of some underground water channel. While in 'faith', I command it to do so, this water will come into Cherith Brook to continue to provide me with water." Elijah could easily have tried to do this, but he didn't.

Let's learn to be very sensitive to the voice of the Holy Spirit like Elijah was.

28
Elisha—A Farmer Who Learnt How To Trust God

The life of Elisha also reveals that we cannot just decide which miracles not specifically promised in the Scriptures we would like to trust God for, without seeking first to find His will.

The first evidence of this is recorded in 2 Kings 2:19-22. Here, we see Elisha trusted God to make the water supply of a mainly ungodly city free of all the foul germs that were causing many deaths, and the women to have miscarriages.

Elisha trusted God to perform this miracle which is recorded in 2 Kings 2:19-22, even though there was no Old Testament Scripture which **specifically promised** that every time an Israelite believer asked God to cleanse a polluted water supply of a mainly ungodly city, that God by a miracle would do it. The Old Testament contains **a general promise** that God would bless the food and water supplies of the Is-raelite nation (see Exodus 23:25). Exodus 23:25 reveals, however, that this promise could only be claimed if most or all Israelites were **putting God first** before anyone or any-thing else.

Elisha could trust God for this miracle only because of one thing. This is revealed in verse 21. Here, Elisha said that God revealed to him that this miracle was His will. 2 Kings 2:19-22 says:

> "Some men from Jericho went to Elisha and said, 'As you know, sir, this is a fine city, but the water is bad and causes miscarriages.' 'Put some salt in a new bowl and bring it to me,' he ordered. They brought it to him, and he went to the spring, threw the salt in the water, and said, 'This is WHAT THE LORD

SAYS: "I make this water pure, and it will not cause
any more deaths or miscarriages.'" And that water has
been pure ever since, just as Elisha said it would be."
                                (Good News Version)

Elisha's attitude of being certain that God would give
him exactly what he trusted God for is seen in 2 Kings
2:22:

"And that water has been pure ever since, just as Elisha
SAID IT WOULD BE."   (Good News Version)

Note in this verse, Elisha didn't say that possibly, or
maybe, the water would be pure. He said that it **would**
become pure. The word "would" here is used in the same
sense of certainty with which Hebrews 11:1 and 1 John
5:14-15 encourage us to trust God.

Note also that Elisha **spoke** out in words what he was
believing for in his heart. Elisha, before Mark 11:23 was
written, understood that faith for a miracle that is God's
will is sometimes expressed **partly** by what a person says. If
a person's words reveal uncertainty that God will do something, then faith for this thing isn't present because *the
mouth SPEAKS what the heart is full of* (see Matthew
12:34, Good News Version).

Elisha didn't try to trust God for a miracle that he may
have preferred. He didn't for example ask that God would
give the town of Jericho a new, stone enclosed model water
supply and drainage system. Probably, some twentieth century Christians, if they had been Elisha, would have tried
to trust God for whatever miracle their human minds
wanted. Instead, Elisha trusted God to perform exactly the
miracle that He revealed was His will for Elisha to request.

OTHER MIRACLES

At another time, the soldiers of Israel, Judah and Edom
ran out of drinking water (see 2 Kings 3:9-20). Over the
years, many people have run out of water, but the Holy
Spirit has not performed a miracle of providing water in a
spectacular way, either because **it wasn't His will;** or the
people **didn't know how to recognize His voice** telling them
this miracle was His will; or they **didn't know how to trust
Him** to perform the miracle that He revealed was His will.

In this instance, it was God's will. Verses 16-17 say:

"This is what THE LORD SAYS: 'Dig ditches all over

183

*this dry stream bed. Even though you will not see any
rain or wind, this stream bed will be filled with water..."*
(Good News Version)

Because it was God's will and Elisha exercised certain
faith that this miracle would happen, God did it (see 2 Kings
3:20).

Just as in the life of Agabus (see Acts 11:27-30), Elisha
was also given a revelation from the Holy Spirit, to tell him
when a famine was coming (see 2 Kings 8:1). As in the case
of Agabus, God revealed this information so Elisha could
tell other believers how God wanted them to cope with the
famine. Elisha told a woman from the town of Shunem that
God wanted her to go to live outside Israel.

A CHILD IS RISEN FROM THE DEAD

Elisha's constant **reliance** upon God's guidance in relation to miracles is also seen in earlier historical events relating to the above-mentioned woman from Shunem. This
woman brought her son to Elisha, after the boy had died
(see 2 Kings 4:18-37).

Here, Elisha is seen to be very interested in knowing
God's guidance about such things. The end of verse 27
reveals this. Elisha said:

"And the Lord has not told me a thing about it."
(Good News Version)

Elisha began to pray to the Lord (see 2 Kings 4:33).
Then not long after, the Lord brought the boy back to life.

In this example, Elisha must have first asked God
whether He wanted Elisha to trust Him to bring the boy back
to life again. Otherwise, this would infer that if every time
Elisha prayed for people to rise from the dead and God
always answered, Elisha could have kept the whole human
race in the Middle East from ever dying permanently, if he
had wanted to. This would be ridiculous. The truth of the
matter is that Elisha only trusted God to perform such miracles **after** God had first revealed to him that it was God's
will for him to pray this way. This is confirmed by Romans
8:26, John 15:7 and 1 John 5:14-15.

OTHER EXAMPLES

There are a number of other examples in Elisha's life

which show that he had learnt the correct way to trust God for miracles.

In 2 Kings 4:42-44, we see that Elisha knew that he could only trust God to ensure that a small amount of food would be able to feed one hundred men in a famine, because God had assured Elisha that this was His will. The last part of verse 43 says:

"...Elisha replied, 'Give it to them to eat, BE-CAUSE THE LORD SAYS that they will eat and still have some left over'."   *(Good News Version)*

Elisha didn't try to trust God to perform this miracle just because he wanted to; he only did this **after** he had obtained the Word of the Lord about it.

We see that Elisha not only knew how to find God's will. He also knew how to trust God with Holy Spirit-inspired faith. Elisha's words in verse 43 show he was **sure** that the miracle would take place. Elisha didn't doubt that the Word of the Lord would come to pass.

His faith is also seen in the fact that he **acted** in a manner which showed that he was **certain** that the miracle would come to pass. Elisha's action which expressed his faith is seen when he told his servant to get them the food to eat. If he was doubting that there would be enough food for the one hundred men, he wouldn't have acted this way.

James 2:18 says:

"But someone will say, 'One person has faith, another has actions.' My answer is, 'Show me how anyone can have faith without actions. I will show you my faith BY MY ACTIONS.'"   *(Good News Version)*

In some of the other miracles which God performed in the lives of Elisha and Elijah, no mention is made of God confirming to them by His Holy Spirit that it was His will for them to trust Him for these miracles. However, this doesn't mean that they trusted Him for these miracles without first hearing a Word of the Lord. Romans 10:17 infers that we can't have Holy Spirit-inspired faith unless we have a Word of the Lord on the matter. Chapter 14, "Biblical Miracles Without A Word of the Lord" gives further details.

Elisha was just a farmer who **learnt** over a number of years how to **recognize** the **inner guidance of the Holy Spirit** and to **know** the **teachings of God's Scriptures;** to **obey** the

185

inner guidance of the Holy Spirit and **the Scriptures** and to **know how to trust God for miracles** that were in agreement with His will. God used this simple farmer greatly because he was willing to learn and do all of these and similar things. In 1 Kings 19:19-21, we see Elisha plowing with a team of oxen which are said, in verse 21, to have been his own. Elisha was not a superman who fell down from heaven to earth. If God could use a simple farmer, He can use any of us. But we must **co-operate** with His work in our lives.

CONCLUSION

If we follow the Biblical principles in this book, we can expect to see miracles in our lives. Hundreds of Christians today are already living in this realm of trusting God for the miracles He wants to perform in their lives.

The number and type of miracles that occur in our lives is **up to God to decide.** But **we can block** the occurrence of some of these in our lives if we don't trust Him the way He requires. Some miracles, however, will occur in our lives whether we have faith for them or not. God performs some miracles purely out of His sovereign will and mercy, regardless of any human faith response.

Let us also avoid praying in presumption, or trying to "earn" miracles or trying to force God to do miracles that are not His will. Let us learn how to pray with God-inspired faith and not with its fleshly imitations.

Let's learn to be like the examples of those people mentioned in this book, who knew how to trust God for miracles.

Bible Study Questions

INSTRUCTIONS

This book contains a number of Bible study questions. These questions are written so that any Bible study, house meeting, cell group or other small group can have a guide for studying the Scriptures which relate to the topics discussed in this book. The questions are also suitable for Bible College or Theological College students to use as assignments.

Your group can study these questions a chapter at a time or in any other amount.

Trust the Lord to reveal the answers to these questions. This book is not your textbook. The Holy Bible is your textbook and source of truth.

CHAPTER 1–GOD'S CHARACTER AND WILL
1. Does God want always **the best** for each of us? If you say, "Yes," can you say honestly that you aim always to ask Him for things He reveals are His will for you?
2. What false ideas about God's character do many people have which encourage them not to ask Him for things that are "according to His will"?

CHAPTER 2–THE IMPORTANCE OF GOD'S WILL
1. Why has God limited the availability of His power to prayer requests based on His will in 99% of cases?
2. To find out His will about what specific miracles He wants us to trust Him for, what must we do?

CHAPTER 3–THE IMPORTANCE OF THE HOLY
      SPIRIT
1. Why is the guidance of the Holy Spirit so important in praying for those miracles not specifically promised in the Scriptures?
2. Will the Holy Spirit ever speak contrary to the teachings of the Scriptures? Give reasons.

CHAPTER 4–COMMIT OUR DECISION-MAKING TO
      HIM
1. What attitudes should we have when waiting upon the Lord, seeking

to know His will about what specific miracles He desires us to trust Him to perform?

2. Why are some Christians in a "Catch-22" situation?

CHAPTER 5–**DO MIRACLES GIVE AUTHORITY TO ONE'S TEACHINGS?**

1. If God has often worked through a certain person to perform miracles, does this mean that everything or almost everything he/she writes, teaches or preaches is inspired by God? Give reasons.

CHAPTER 6–**PRAYERS OF PRESUMPTION**

1. What is presumption prayer?
2. What verses of Scripture are interpreted by some Christian authors in ways that are contrary to the plain meaning of other verses - leading many to pray in presumption?
3. How is it possible to treat God like a "big spiritual Santa Claus"?
4. When is thinking, mentally picturing and saying that God will perform a miracle of use?
5. How was Jesus tempted by Satan to pray in presumption?
6. The Scriptures record the disciples James and John asking for miracles presumptuously in two situations. These are recorded in Luke 9:53-56 and Mark 10:35-45. Explain why their requests in these situations were not faith, but presumption.

CHAPTER 7–**PRESUMPTION OR FAITH?**

1. Did the Apostle Peter act in faith or presumption when he began to walk on water, as recorded in Matthew 14:22-32? Give reasons.
2. What is pseudo-faith?

CHAPTER 8–**PRESUMPTION OR GOD'S WILL?**

1. What does John 14:14 mean? How is this verse commonly misinterpreted?
2. How is it possible to use the Name of Jesus as a magical formula or a pagan chant?
3. What does Psalm 37:4 mean?
4. What is the danger in the popular teaching that God will give us whatever we dream and trust Him to fulfil?
5. What is a neglected aspect of the popular teaching about "the God-kind of faith"?

CHAPTER 9–**ASKING OUTSIDE OF GOD'S WILL**

1. What were the results when God gave the people of Israel a king when they asked, even though it was not His perfect will (see 1 Samuel 8:1-22)?
2. What lessons can we learn from Numbers Chapter 22, 2 Peter 2:15-16, Jude 11, Numbers 31:15-16 and Revelation 2:14 taken together?

CHAPTER 10–**GOD'S WILL IS BEST**

1. Does God give us **always** only what **specifically** we ask of Him? Or does God give us sometimes something better than what we ask? Give some Scriptural examples of this.

Bible Study Questions

CHAPTER 11–DIFFERENCE BETWEEN NATURAL AND BIBLICAL FAITH

1. What is the difference between natural and Biblical faith?
2. Do non-Christians have Biblical faith? Give reasons.
3. Is it possible to worship faith instead of God? Give reasons.
4. How can we co-operate with the Lord Jesus living within us in His performance of miracles?
5. If I cursed a fig tree while believing and confessing God would wither it, without Him guiding me specifically to do this, would He wither it?

CHAPTER 12–RARE INSTANCES IN SCRIPTURE

1. What two types of situations can we observe in the Scriptures of God being willing to answer a prayer request that is contrary to what originally was His will? How common are these?
2. What does Abraham's intercession for Sodom and Gomorrah teach us about intercession?
3. What does 2 Chronicles 1:7-12 reveal?

CHAPTER 13–TRUE INTERCESSION

1. What do Jeremiah 7:16 and Jeremiah's response to God's Word spoken in this verse, teach us?

CHAPTER 14–BIBLICAL MIRACLES WITHOUT A WORD OF THE LORD

1. If we read 2 Chronicles Chapter 32 alone and did not take into account other passages of Scripture which speak of the same historical events, how could we get a wrong impression of what occurred?

CHAPTER 15–GOD HAS NO FAVOURITES

1. Do 1 John 3:21-22 and 1 Peter 3:7 teach that we have to reach a special level of "holiness" or "worthiness" before God will answer our requests for miracles? Give reasons.
2. Does God love the Apostles and Prophets more than He loves you?
3. What does Galatians 3:5 reveal about God performing miracles?
4. Why does God wish to perform miracles for us?
5. Why has God performed relatively more miracles for the Apostles, Prophets and some devoted Christians over the centuries than He has for millions of other Christians?
6. How can a false sense of unworthiness affect our expectation that God may perform miracles for us?
7. What does James 5:17 reveal about praying for miracles?

CHAPTER 16–GOD DID NOT ANSWER THE REQUEST OF THE MOST HUMBLE HOLY PERSON

1. Considering what Numbers 12:3 and Deuteronomy 34:10-12 reveal about Moses, why does Deuteronomy 3:23-27 say what it does about Moses' prayer request?

CHAPTER 17–WE CANNOT EARN MIRACLES

1. Can we force God to perform a miracle that is not His will for us by positively thinking, positively confessing and mentally picturing (or visualising) it long enough?
2. In the Bible, miracles are seen to be acts of God's grace. In the New

Testament, what does the word "grace" mean?

3. Romans Chapter 4 is concerned primarily with showing that Abraham did not earn his salvation. But what also does it reveal about trusting God for miracles not specifically promised in the Bible to all believers?

4. Do we "earn" miracles by our faith? Or is faith the means by which we accept or receive humbly what God desires to do for us? Give reasons.

5. Why do humans find it so hard to understand that we cannot "earn" miracles from God by any means?

6. Are our thoughts, words and actions of no value in trusting God to perform miracles that are His will? Give reasons.

7. If we praise and thank God enough, will He do whatever we ask? Give reasons.

8. Does the parable of the unrighteous judge (see Luke 18:1-8) reveal that if we ask God in prayer for something enough times, He will "reward" our persistence and give us what we want? Give reasons.

9. What other formulas do many Roman Catholic and Orthodox church-goers use to try to supposedly "earn" answers to their requests to God for miracles?

CHAPTER 18—JAMES 5:16

1. What does the second part of James 5:16 teach us?

CHAPTER 19—WHAT IS THE BIBLICAL TYPE OF FAITH?

1. Does faith in God mainly relate to receiving miracles from God? If not, to what else does faith in God relate?

2. What does Hebrews 11:1 teach us about Biblical faith?

3. What does 1 John 5:14-15 teach about trusting God for miracles?

CHAPTER 20—FAITH RESPONSE

1. Has God decided to limit some of the manifestations of His miracle-working power to the degree that we allow Holy Spirit- inspired faith to be expressed through our minds and spirits? Give Scriptural evidence to support your answer.

2. Why did the prophet Daniel pray and trust God to help the Jews rebuild Jerusalem and their nation, after they had been many years in captivity when He had already revealed that this was His will?

3. Is it God or faith that performs miracles?

CHAPTER 21—THE SOVEREIGNTY OF GOD

1. "God will only do things in His physical creation and in the affairs of mankind if someone prays, asking Him to do these things, and/or someone exercises faith, trusting Him to do these things. When Adam sinned, he passed the rulership of this world to Satan, and as a result, God cannot legally interfere in the affairs of His physical creation." Discuss.

2. Why has God in some instances decided to limit the manifestation of His miracle-working power to whether someone trusts Him to do what He has revealed specifically is His will?

3. Why is it wrong to have a hyper-Calvinistic over-emphasis on the place of the Sovereignty of God in His performing of miracles?

191

Bible Study Questions

4. What do Luke 1:5-25, Luke 8:22-25 and Matthew 14:22-33 reveal to us about God performing miracles?

CHAPTER 22 — WHEN WE DON'T KNOW HIS WILL

1. When the Scriptures do not reveal whether it is God the Father's will to ask for a particular miracle and His Spirit has not given specific guidance, what should we do?
2. When we don't know whether a specific miracle is God's will, why is it wrong to add merely the words "if it be Thy will" on to the end of our request for a specific miracle?

CHAPTER 23 — MIRACLES REQUIRING HOLY SPIRIT REVELATION

1. List 10 examples of miracles that the Bible does not promise specifically to all believers and which we can only be sure will occur if the Holy Spirit reveals these are the Father's will.

CHAPTER 24 — MOSES — A GREAT EXAMPLE

1. List 10 examples of Moses receiving guidance from God which revealed what specific miracles He wanted Moses to trust Him for and then Moses trusting Him to perform these miracles.
2. Why is obedience to the Holy Spirit's guidance so important in trusting God to perform miracles?
3. Was Moses certain that the specific miracles God showed were His will, would occur? Or did he add to his prayer requests in these instances the words "if it be Thy will"?

CHAPTER 25 — JOSHUA

1. What Biblical principles of faith do we see:
   a) when Joshua trusted God to stop the fast-flowing Jordan River?
   b) when Joshua and many of the people of Israel trusted God to knock down the walls of the city of Jericho?

CHAPTER 26 — DANIEL

1. How could the prophet Daniel be certain that miraculously God would help many of the Jews, who had been captive in Babylon for many years, to rebuild Jerusalem and God's Temple?

CHAPTER 27 — ELIJAH

1. What can we learn from Elijah's life about praying for miracles not specifically promised in the Scriptures to all believers?

CHAPTER 28 — ELISHA — A FARMER WHO LEARNT HOW TO TRUST GOD

1. What lessons do 2 Kings 2:19-22, 3:9-20 and 4:42-44 reveal about how Elisha trusted God to perform miracles not promised specifically in the Scriptures?